Bardsy

Publishable Characters:
A Complete Guide with Tests & Comprehensive Developer

Adam F. Simon, PhD

23371 Mulholland Drive Suite #446 Woodland Hills, CA 91364

info@bardsy.com

Published in the United States by Bardsy Press

Correspondence regarding the content of this book should be sent to Bardsy, Inc., Editorial Department, at the above address.

Publishers: Celeste Davidson and Adam F. Simon

Executive Editor: Celeste Davidson

Managing Editor: Alex Thieme

Acquisitions Editor: Pamela Raleigh

Graphic Designer: Aaron Weiss

Printed in 2025

www.bardsy.com

ABOUT BARDSY

Bardsy helps serious writers produce compelling novels.

Our experienced authors and educators offer a well-researched and thoroughly tested approach to guide and support your efforts. Each part springs from a unified set of ideas, tools and resources, which are firmly rooted in reader psychology.

We feature workshops, courses, regular anthology contests and published guides as well as our curated community. With our help, your story will captivate agents, publishers, and readers.

Celeste and Adam founded Bardsy as an alternative to writing sites that bombard talented writers with false hope, gimmicks and little else. Their passion for great storytelling and compassion for other writers, as well as abundant experience in publishing and academia, led to the creation of a writing program that actually works. Bardsy's unique, research-proven method provides support to writers at every step of the process, from that first, lightbulb moment to a completed manuscript, and beyond.

Celeste Davidson is the best-selling author of Who Was William Shakespeare? (Grosset & Dunlap) and One Leaf Rides the Wind (Viking), and several other award-winning titles, including Julia Morgan Built a Castle (Viking), Snapshots: The Wonders of Monterey Bay (Viking) and The Queen's Progress (Viking), having sold over 600,000 copies, to date.

She has taught creative writing and English literature for over twenty years. Her students know that she speaks from experience, and see her as an empathetic model who offers advice likely to multiply their chances of success.

MIT drop-out, UCLA Ph.D. and former Yale visiting professor, Adam Simon is the author of The Winning Message (Cambridge University Press), Mass Informed Consent (Rowman and Littlefield) and over a dozen peer reviewed social science articles, as well as Bardsy's Social Media Primer with Alex Thieme.

Among his awards are a NSF Graduate Fellowship and a share of a MacArthur Award for Creative and Effective Institutions. He is known for commitment to his students' success and devotion to coherent storytelling, not to mention an all-consuming love of science fiction and empirical research.

ACKNOWLEDGEMENTS

The importance of having a strong community to support your writing cannot be emphasized enough. I want to express my boundless gratitude to the members of the Bardsy community who contributed their time and knowledge to this endeavor.

Pamela Raleigh: thank you so much for your willingness to read (and re-read), patiently offer insightful feedback and pinpoint areas of confusion or mess. This work would not have been completed without you. Huge thank yous to Celeste Davidson and Alex Thieme for their contributions to Bardsy in general and to supporting this work in particular.

My gratitude extends to the members of my directed writing groups, whose responses to inchoate ideas led to the clearer presentation you, hopefully, see. Many thanks also to Ava Dumas and Aiesha Eser for guiding this work to market. And, a final thanks to Aaron Weiss for another fantastic design and publication effort.

We all hope reading this will benefit your work.

This book is dedicated to Rosa Aguilar, my life's most treasured gift.

Adam

TABLE OF CONTENTS

6 **Chapter 1**
Introduction and Preview

12 **Chapter 2**
Significance: Why Characters Make (or Break) Your Novel

22 **Chapter 3**
Prerequisite: Understand Great Fictional Beings are Authentic and Investable People

46 **Chapter 4**
Co-Creation: Embrace Your Readers as Junior Partners

58 **Chapter 5**
Coherence: Evaluate Your Characters in Context with the MCS and PI

78 **Chapter 6**
Description: Compose your Complex, Integrated Being

104 **Chapter 7**
Backstory: Let Readers Bring Your Character to Life

124 **Chapter 8**
Agency: Build Their Lives in Your Story

158 **Chapter 9**
Comprehensive Character Developer

Chapter 01

Introduction & Preview

PREVIEW:

1. Your success starts with winning one reader's love through your characters.

2. *Publishable* characters are authentic (feel real) and investible (worth knowing)

3. Each is a carefully constructed, fully integrated individual who follows no formula.

4. Readers use simulacra (mental models) to relate to them as real people.

5. Properly testing your beings on actual readers is extremely worthwhile.

6. Don't use this guide's Comprehensive Character Developer before reading every chapter.

Introduction

Your authorial success begins when one reader organically finds your work and loves — not likes — it. Winning that first love is the most difficult creative challenge you'll face; yet, it's been done. You've seen the proof in reading your favorite novels. Storytellers (AI be damned) will continue to find adoring fans so long as humans exist. Writing compelling characters provides the surest way for you to win that affection.

So, what makes a character compelling? Two somewhat opposing criteria stand out. First, authenticity: your characters must be knowable in the same way as actual people. Second: investment, your characters must be worth getting to know. We rarely meet truly interesting people in everyday life, even though they are all, by definition, authentic because they actually exist. Readers expect more from than authenticity from your fictional beings. They'll only spend time and money on creations that continually capture their attention. Thus, great authors balance these two requirements, offering fascinating beings with more than a toe grounded in reality. The payoff is clear; compelling characters lead to an imagined realness that makes reading worthwhile. Part of this reward takes the form of grokking, extreme empathy between reader and character.

Here's the thing: great characters follow no formula. It's ridiculous to believe that filling in a template, doing random exercises or creating an extensive backstory will guarantee success.

Instead, this guide builds from a simple premise. To write great characters, you must begin by understanding how readers, including your potential fan, relate to effective fictional beings. Spoiler alert: they think of them as real people. More specifically, reading prompts an audience to recreate your beings in their heads. These recreations, called simulacra, are functionally identical to the ones used for anyone else they know. Remember that word: simulacrum; it's this guide's most important. How well you manage readers' simulacra largely determines your characters' success. The do's and dont's of character creation follow from this remarkable fact — to repeat: readers relate to *publishable* fictional characters as real people. Science can help us understand these relationships, so we'll discuss it when appropriate. For example, science (not to mention common sense) teaches that your characters' success depends on continually building readers' simulacrum in a way that increases their familiarity and promotes empathy. It also teaches that the right words can induce readers to augment your details with their own knowledge and experience. For example, you can take advantage of archetypes to generate a mostly fleshed out being in relatively few words. On the other hand, this guide pointedly does not offer a "science" of storytelling. We'll discuss research only where it's immediately applicable and vital to understanding the topic.

Overall, readers' natural reactions to your characters governs the degree of your success. This guide offers specific tests, which assess whether your characters are effective, i.e. they contribute to story satisfaction, for this reason. As you've heard, failure is the best teacher. Nobody can offer anything better for your writing than good tests, which help you see how actual readers respond. Many authors, for instance, are surprised when they witness an unexpected response, such as a misaligned fact or an unintended feeling, to their supposedly perfect introduction. Reading this guide will be infinitely more helpful if you follow up and apply these checks to your writing. Keep in mind that they don't test the reader. They assess how well you're doing your job as an author. So, use them to test yourself, particularly that you transmit — more your being from your brain to the reader's — well. Put another way, this feedback gauges how well you're doing as well as what you may need to change or add.

This guide features a comprehensive character development system at the end. Of course, it's the deepest and most thorough template we've seen; nevertheless, use it only after you're familiar with the entire guide, including its tests. Don't expect it to create your characters for you, even if the online, interactive version is amazing.

Guide Outline and Chapter Preview

This guide, *Publishable Characters*, contains eight chapters, which are followed by Bardsy's Comprehensive Character Developer (CCD). Please read the chapters — in order — before using the developer. While you can skim or flip to the last page, it's less likely that you'll produce a *publishable* character without applying the techniques this guide explains. A quick plug: an interactive version of the CCD, with a printable sheet and character archive, is at https://bardsy.com/character

The chapters are divided into two parts. Two through five establish an understanding of what goes into writing characters.

- **Chapter 2** pinpoints your goal, a deep reader empathy called grokking, by examining the novel's history and purpose. Put simply, novels that prompt grokking are compelling while the rest fall short.

- **Chapter 3** establishes two criteria: authenticity and investability. Evidence suggests that readers relate to fictional characters and real people in the same way. This remarkable truth stems from mental models called simulcra, which we use — nearly interchangeably — for both kinds of beings. It reveals that crafting authentic beings comes easily because everyone you meet, including nearly all fictional characters, exist. It's much harder to attract readers' investment. This chapter covers how to earn that attention, and ends with the "retelling" test, which tracks your progress toward meeting the challenge.

- **Chapter 4** details Co-Creation, how readers come to know and love your characters as they fill in whatever blanks you leave, which makes the audience a partner in your novel's experience. You provide the seeds, enough relevant detail to get them started and keep going, and they do the rest. Among other things, they add cultural knowledge, like stereotypes and archetypes, to the beings you create. Managing this process well leads to success.

- **Chapter 5** addresses coherence, the essential synergy between your characters, world, conflict, theme and plot. The need for coherence prevents examining characters in isolation, only in context. It offers two tools to check coherence as and after you write. First, the Minimum Complete Story (MCS) is a short, yet complete, version of your story, which provides both compass and ruler. Regularly saying it aloud helps you develop your story even as it aligns each day's work with the big picture (and it may alleviate writer's block). Second, the Publishability Index™ (PI), is a comprehensive 23-item checklist covering every aspect of a story. Use it to holistically evaluate chapters as well as whole novels. The PI also provides the basis for developing, presenting, and nurturing your characters that this guide's remainder explains.

The final three chapters implement this understanding step by step, starting with character creation, moving to their introduction and concluding with a discussion of how to nurture them as they live in your reader's mind.

- **Chapter 6** shows how to create a complex, integrated being in two steps: composition and blending. It offers a three-part "Character Equation" that draws on yourself, cultural knowledge, like stereotypes, and aspects of people you know (referents). After an extended example, it describes exercises that integrate these ingredients into a whole being through repeated interactions. The more your image of the being solidifies, the easier and more organic your writing becomes.

- **Chapter 7** lays out the proper use of backstory and lays out how to introduce your beings. It explores the dynamics of all human relations and shares tips on making written intros successful. This discussion concludes with the "gossip" test, which gauges the story relevance of details.

- **Chapter 8** shows how your characters live — in the reader's minds — through the identities and choices you construct. It outlines the mental process, aka Golden Chain, that allows situations to produce empathy. Then, it explains how to link choice situations into compelling plots and meaningful character arcs, the value you must deliver to satisfy your audience.

Chapter 02

Significance: Why Characters Make (or Break) Your Novel

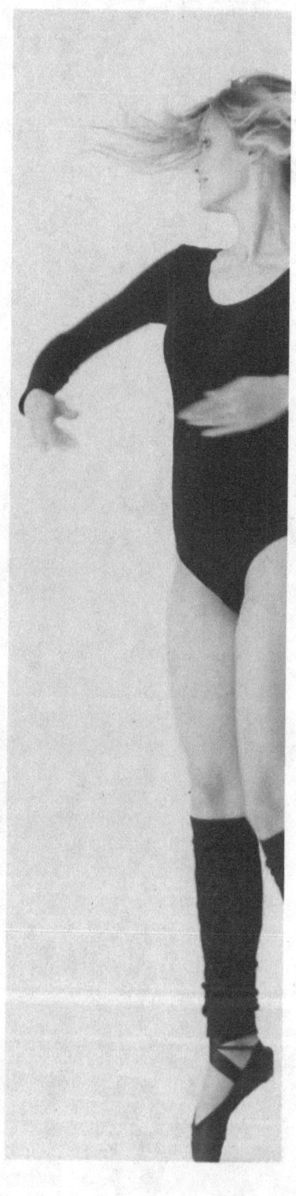

PREVIEW:

1. Cervantes' use of inner dialogue invented the novel as we know it.

2. This key literary device fosters a deep empathy, called grokking, that merges character and reader.

3. Successful novels depend on grokking to explore psychological issues and provide meaning.

4. A scientific approach to reading, like seeing how mirror neurons promote empathy, helps your writing.

5. Our natural interest in others makes Character-Driven stories easier to write (and read).

Cervantes Invents the Novel

You've heard of *Don Quixote*. You may also know that this fame comes from his eponymous novel's unparalleled success — probably, the first bestselling novel. Published in 1605, *Don Quixote* quickly required ever larger printings and translations to meet eager readers' demands. While the advent of the printing press had recently reshaped the marketplace, Miguel de Cervantes won this popularity through a singular innovation, which we generally know as inner dialogue. This literary technique transforms storytelling by changing the focus from events to people, a shift that multiplies the opportunities for profound explorations. In so doing, *Don Quixote* set the pattern for every subsequent novel. Likewise, this novel demonstrates the centrality of character and its importance to your success.

Estimates suggest *Don Quixote* has sold 500 million copies in over a thousand editions, translated into every major language. It gave birth to mass piracy, unauthorized sequels and copyright laws, as well. In a time when few could read, copies of *Don Quixote* made their way around the world. People were mesmerized by the tale. To recap for those unfamiliar with his story, this low-born man falls into fantasy, believing he's a knight, after reading too many chivalric adventures. *Don Quixote* becomes the star of his own imaginary story as the delusional reshapes his world: prostitutes to ladies, inns to castles, windmills to monsters. Meanwhile, in the real world, his attempts at nobility embarrass his companions and amuse bystanders. Even if you haven't read the book, you know him. He's enmeshed in our culture as an archetype; his name labels people with similar natures. The Don is quixotic, a somewhat foolishly ambitious dreamer.

Inner Dialogue Unlocks Success

Why did *Don Quixote* do so much better than everything that came before? Cervantes' success can be traced to a new literary technique, one that opened a window into character's minds that few readers can resist. Specifically, Cervantes introduced what most call inner dialogue. Readers experience the character's internal state of mind through the characters' self-talk. This vicariousness prompts an empathic merge, where readers step into a fictional being's shoes and enter their minds. Put another way, this access provokes a deep empathy, which we'll call grokking

This innovation revolutionized storytelling. No longer a campfire legend or a declamatory ballad, the novel's events become just another day in the character's life, albeit in the fantastical world he inhabits. And, more importantly, we get to join him; empathy allows us to experience his day as he does. Deep empathy, then, goes a step further, it allows us to become him and vicariously live these experiences as ourselves. On another level, access to Quixote's thoughts provides additional information. It adds whatever he sees to whatever else we know about the situation. A windmill is not a windmill; it's a monster, for example. Inner dialogue morphs readers into the Don, leading to the deep empathy necessary to appreciate that attacking a windmill is a noble attempt to save the village.

Were he merely a simpleton to be mocked, Cervantes' character would generate cheap laughs but little sympathy. Instead, this literary device compels us to join the delusion, which makes his Don more than an idiot in shabby armor. No longer a one-dimensional nuisance; we know *Don Quixote* because we are him, people struggling to do good within our limited worldview.

Inner dialogue doesn't seem special to us because it's so familiar. We read this kind of self-talk in words and take it to be ordinary dialogue. It simply mirrors the way we talk, often silently, to ourselves. That fact doesn't diminish its power; far from it, its ubiquity proclaims its importance. Cervantes' use of this device transformed the Don (and eventually your character) from an object to observe into a relatable being, one with thoughts and feelings like everyone else. In other words, direct mental access brings him to life. Talk to anyone versed in this novel; they speak of him like an eccentric neighbor or crazy relative, not a distant, historical figure. Further, they're easily able to gossip about him and his activities.

Before *Don Quixote*, readers could only know characters by what they did, much like how we experience actors' portrayals in movies. When watching movies, one thing to notice is that they generally avoid using voiceovers to reveal what's running through the characters' minds. We only know the players by what we see or hear them do. Novels, in contrast, can be seen to be all about the voiceover. It's amazing what this technique allows. Inner dialogue means readers aren't limited to witnessing stories in the third person. Reading a novel isn't a tame safari, where you have to keep your hands inside the vehicle. Instead, you're there. You vicariously experience the adventure he does. Cervantes' use of inner dialogue makes reading *Don Quixote* exciting not only through spectacle but through deep empathy, the grokking that merges reader and character. By reading his mind, you charge the windmills even as you join others watching him make a fool of himself.

Inner dialogue — and the vicariousness it brings — points to the written word's prime advantage over other media. Revealing hidden thought in other media tends to be limited, awkward, heavy handed or all of the above. The presence of self-talk, in fact, distinguishes novels (and derivatives) from other literary forms. Of course, you don't need to use inner dialogue, but leaving it out is risky; such writing may actually fall short of being a novel, let alone a great story. One takeaway from *Don Quixote*'s success is that you must take advantage of this route to winning our readers' love. Beyond that it leads to insights regarding what makes characters, and novels, *publishable.*

Novels are Psychological Studies

The primacy of inner dialogue points to the fact that great novels revolve around their characters' mental state. This focus — on thoughts, feelings and their effect on behavior — immerses readers in fictional yet human experiences. Moreover, the better the novel, the less the inner dialogue connection resembles some "shrink" leaning back on a chair couch, taking notes. With proper execution, the reader leans into the story to the point they fall in. This linkage allows the merged reader / character (yes, it's a bit magical) to retain their humanity in facing situations beyond anything we could hope to encounter, let alone imagine, without your wizardry. Similarly, it gives novels a unique capacity to enrich readers' connection to and understanding of others, not to mention of themselves. Their popularity largely comes from fulfilling this function., These observations, taken together, teach us that novels are psychological studies at heart (or such studies are crappy novels). We look and return to them for significant experiences, which reveal something about the mystery of life. In short, great novels satisfy our need to answer the fundamental question about human behavior: why?

Why didn't someone call after a fantastic first date? Or, if you're feeling deep, why do bad things happen to good people? It's impossible to answer questions like these definitively. On the other hand, we don't give up. We're endlessly curious about others and the reasons they do what they do. Many — your potential fans — turn to novels in this quest. Our endless speculations may or may not bear fruit in actual life. Not so in well-crafted stories; ultimately, everything is comprehensible; a satisfying novel rewards every guess with a "correct" answer. Keep this in mind: whenever you introduce a character, have them make a choice or describe how they make coffee, your reader (usually subconsciously) tries to figure out what's going on. In this way, novels succeed when the reader walks away with a richer view of their world.

This insight paints a big target on your overarching task: to write a story that sheds a diffuse light on humanity, one which assists readers' search for meaning. This goal makes creating effective characters absolutely essential. Readers enter your story through them. You want them to face the same challenges, make choices and suffer consequences with them. Your career depends on linking potential fans to your main characters. When you've done your job, readers live these experiences as their own. And, they love doing this and reward you with the adoration great authors deserve.

We often call this special connection engagement. Engagement, however, has become a buzzword, overly synonymous with great. This makes it vague, unusable as a way to begin a discussion of *publishable* characters. You need a clear target; one that's easy to define and which happens to cover what most mean when they say engagement. Surrogacy doesn't quite work; it implies a substitute or replacement and, thus, keeps the distance between reader and character. Grokking, on the other hand, fits this bill.

Grokking is Your Goal

To grok, a provocative term borrowed from science fiction grand master Robert Heinlien, is to empathize so deeply with another being that you "merge" into one. Think of the love songs, such as "Two Hearts," one mind. It's what Cervantes achieved between ardent readers and his Don. Granted, it's difficult to reach this highest level of interpersonal linkage, perfect empathy. Nevertheless, you should unrelentingly pursue it. Reaching this state signals your characters have gone above and beyond in terms of contributing to your novel's success. This guide continually returns to this motif, namely that fostering empathy means that the reactions your characters elicit are identical to the responses real people trigger.

Empathy's consequences make it a worthy goal. Building relationships and fostering understanding depend on it. It's a move toward taking another's perspective, the aforementioned stepping into another's shoes. Many social theorists regard these feelings as the glue holding society together. This significance has motivated many to study empathy scientifically. Before opening the door to science (and to encourage authors who find it less savory), we need to talk about what science can teach authors.

The premise is simple: it helps to understand something about how minds work for you to write successful stories, ones that synergize with brains. Equivalently stated: stories that succeed do so because they take advantage of how our minds work. You could rediscover this knowledge through trial and error, read more technical works that convey said wisdom or you can learn and apply a few fundamental findings concerning how humans relate to others. Hopefully, you'll choose the last option, and stick with this guide. Of course, some in the writing community disdain science. Little can be said to outright rejectors. The sole claim here is that good scientific research can inform your writing. It, for instance, describes exactly how readers relate to fictional characters. Your natural curiosity and motivation to write better provides enough motivation to keep an open mind with respect to these facts to see if they'll aid our work.

Using Science to Write More Effectively

Let's digress slightly to clarify an important point: there is no "science" of storytelling, a singular formula for writing compelling novels. Humans and stories go way back; nothing can compete with these millennia of trial and error, which have produced voluminous contemporary storytelling advice. This history strongly suggests that any novel approach to storytelling, perhaps some new insight, is either not really new or likely to fall short. In place of an all encompassing science, which dictates everything you should do, this guide offers selected scientific insights covering how people relate to others and, then, applies those insights to how readers relate to fictional beings (like yours). There's no magic; the science merely expands and deepens your creative process in areas you probably already want to do. In so doing, this guide pushes you toward reaching your desired outcome, winning readers' love.

Some Science Worth Using: Testing

Speaking of science, it provides something beyond knowledge; you've heard of it: the scientific method. We won't go into detail here, save to emphasize one piece you absolutely, positively must use: testing. When it comes to writing, evaluating your work is a must; it's the only way to determine whether you've really satisfied your reader; it also tracks your progress toward that goal. Put bluntly, getting precise and actionable feedback is the most effective way to improve your characters; therefore, you should regularly examine how audiences respond to them. Most importantly, your assessments should apply the retelling procedure this guide describes below. This method concentrates on what they take from your words and nothing else. Any other way to get feedback is less direct and, thus, suspect.

Why testing? A surprisingly large number of authors don't really consider readers as they write. Maybe that's not as bad as making erroneous assumptions about your readership. Either way, getting to know readers by witnessing how they react to your words is absolutely essential. You may, for instance, believe you've made a perfect introduction, but only testing will let you know for sure. Similarly, seeing a volunteer draw unexpected conclusions about your being's nature is eye opening. For this reason, this guide regularly presents precise tests. These assessments center on confirming you've accomplished the task at hand. If you've fallen short, they'll also assist in pinpointing the shortcomings. Use them, repeatedly, to assess your writing's effectiveness. The results are certain to surprise you.

The Science of Empathy

Let's bring in a pinch of neuroscience to cement our appreciation of empathy. This term, to be precise, refers to an emotional overlap between two beings (typically human, sometimes other), call it a sensitivity to others' feelings. You experience it everyday: the urge to yawn after others do. When a passerby stubs their toe, you get a youch — a physical reflex. Yet, this reflex can't really be physical, it's not your toe! Whenever you witness joy, grief, worry, irritation or astonishment, to name a few, you feel those emotions, respectively. Humans catch, like a contagion, every emotion that pops up in social situations. Empathy also differs from sympathy; it requires an overlap of experience, roughly feeling the same emotion. It is remarkable: though neurologically indistinguishable, empathic emotions are triggered indirectly. That's the definition of vicarious: the experience occurs courtesy of another being. Crucially, this feeling also arises when you see videos (google Homer Simpson's football to the groin), and when you read. Let's repeat this finding: readers experience the same emotions as your characters (if you do your job well).

Here's the science. There's a brain function behind empathic reactions. This neurobiology (a great word) uses "mirror" neurons; these cells empower us to imitate the feelings we observe in others. They fire whenever we notice another's emotion; moreover this activation happens in the same brain area our own emotions use. The name is apt. The feeling we get is the same as if our own circumstances caused it. Bingo; that's it. If you hadn't heard about mirror neurons, now you know a bit more about how empathy works. This phenomenon, which was first seen by ancients (their writings cover almost every aspect of humanity), has a scientifically demonstrated mechanism — something our brains physically do. You might, for instance, imagine triggering these microscopic cells as you write.

When it comes to your characters you should see empathy as a ladder, with grokking, a deep empathic merging, at the top. Ignoring sits at the bottom, not even on the lowest rung. The "talking to a wall" expression suits. At the lowest rung, a reader may recognize "something like that happened to me, too." or see a piece of themselves in your beings. The similarity isn't exact, but it's a start. We're going to focus on that and how to entice (or push) readers to climb higher. Grokking, the highest rung, is the opposite of ignoring. The boundary between readers and character dissolves, achieving the discussed merge. Barely cognizant of words, they forget they're reading. With concentration so intense, an interruption will startle. The merge literally brings your character to life. And, as character and reader exist in each other, they live your story. Perhaps an impossible goal, then again we're taking our cue from *Don Quixote* — better to aim high and miss than settle for something less.

Character-Driven Novels are Easier to Write

Thinking about empathy, mirror neurons and grokking might make writing great characters seem difficult. Nothing could be further from the truth. This background just details the way our brains already work; we meet, get to know and feel for others all the time. Once in a while, we grok them. The hard part is getting readers to apply these natural, everyday processes to your work, so hard that it will take this entire guide to detail how to reach this goal. Let's take a moment (to build confidence and) to go over how these social processes' accessibility make Character-Driven novels less challenging to write.

Humans have a natural inclination to want to learn about other people, why they are the way they are and do what they do. Think about the last time you indulged in gossip. Despite the conventional view that it has malign overtones, gossiping centers on investigating or transmitting important social information: why people do what they do or are the way that they are. *Who* would do something so wild? *Why* would they do it? We want answers; answers that come in story form. Due to simple curiosity, or something selfish, these stories command our interest. All stories need characters, those that put characters first are the ones that readers naturally want most.

Defining Story Relative to Character

We at Bardsy define a story as a coherent combination of five familiar elements: character, world, plot, conflict and theme. To preview later discussion: coherence is key; a well-crafted story five elements are fully developed and synchronized for maximal impact. Failing to coherently combine these elements means whatever you write isn't a story and can't compel readers. Of these five elements, character stands apart from the rest. Some might put plot first in terms of reading and writing. They would point to the claims many make, reading to "see how it ends," for example. But, having read once, surely we know a story's twists and turns, including the end.

Now consider how readers treat cherished novels, lavishing hours on them from start to finish, over and over again. People read their favorite book dozens or hundreds of times. If you ask, they'll say rereading gives the same pleasure, if not more, as the first time. Otherwise, they'd stop. Any interest plot holds on subsequent reads comes from the reader character link. The attraction comes from being in the moment, co-experiencing the story. Applying the same logic to the other elements would affirm this wisdom: character comes first.

Relative to other elements, character offers the smoothest path to start and keep writing. As an author, you have a greater than normal interest in the human condition. At the same time, you have equal access to a lifetime of social interaction. There's opportunity in every person you've met; each offers a starting point for possible protagonists and villains. (We'll talk more about using these memories.) The innumerable hours you've spent observing and talking to others provides a template for your characters' actions. Infusing your creations with this expertise makes them effective — the reader accepts them as people. What do you do when you meet an interesting new person? Typically, you aim to get along. Your social faculty kicks in, you get to know them and a connection forms. This almost instinctual process applies to reading. These social capabilities and encyclopedic knowledge of people, which you and readers share, give character an endowment that other story elements can't match.

Chapter 03

Prerequisite: Understand Great Fictional Beings are Authentic and Investable People

PREVIEW:

1. Mental models (simulacra) make relating to other beings, including fictional characters, possible.

2. Spinning up simulacra, which is easy, makes beings authentic — our first criteria.

3. Expanding simulacra is hard, meaning you should focus on investment — our second criteria.

4. Retelling collects the best feedback and can test for these prerequisites.

5. Your quest for deep empathy starts with identities and situations that earn an initial investment.

6. Avoid confusion and boredom; really, avoid them as they lead readers to drop your novel.

How does a reader actually experience fictional characters? This question sets up your challenge and establishes this guide's premise. The answer comes from the study of person perception, an area of neuroscience and social psychology that details the mental processes we use to relate to other human beings. This understanding, then, leads to two criteria — authenticity and investability — that supports developing and evaluating the beings you create.

Humans Relate to Others Through Simulacra

What makes a person real? To begin answering this question, list the people you know. Friends and family come first, your partner, mom and BFF. Next come acquaintances, coworkers or neighbors. Then, there are people you recognize but don't know well, your letter carrier or bank teller. At some point, you'll think about people you've never met, celebrities, the President or famous authors. You kind of know them — to the extent you ever know anyone — what they're like, who they're dating and more. Squinting a bit extends this familiarity to historical figures. With enough biography, we're familiar enough to say we "know" Abraham Lincoln, Queen Elizabeth or Elvis. Keep going.

A tiny leap takes you to fictional characters. Like Lincoln, you could claim to know your favorite literary persons, such as Spiderman or Elizabeth Bennett, and few would object. You know them in this sense: you can easily describe them, talk about what they've done (and why), then — most importantly — make well-supported guesses as to their reactions to new challenges. For example, how Spiderman would deal with a new villain or who'd be the ideal match for Elizabeth. These guesses could go beyond their specific domain; for example, who could date Spidey or antagonize Elizabeth. Past that, you're able to imagine how they'd respond to a new film or feel about current events. These guesses might be off the mark, but you could still back them up and gossip about these fictional beings as if they were real. Crucially, this ability to blabber on about others suggests we see them as distinct personalities with all that entails. This realness comes from knowledge. It's knowing them (or about them) that makes them real to us.

Simulacra Store Knowledge to Predict Behavior

Science unequivocally reveals that we store knowledge about beings in mental models that simulate them. These recreations — called simulacra — start as undifferentiated person-shaped blobs, instantaneously "spun up" when we encounter, including reading about, anyone new. We quickly refine them based on salient details, like height, cultural codes and more. These simulations aren't perfect. Like all models, they are approximations. Select simulacra, however, become richer and more accurate with exposure and interest. The more time (and attention) spent with someone, the more detailed your corresponding model of them becomes. In simple terms: you know them better. Someone you meet briefly while shopping stays pretty blob-like; on the other hand, your best friend's or spouse's simulacrum is painstakingly detailed, reflecting years of interactions and thought. You undoubtedly have an elaborate imago of your favorite character, as well. At bottom, we know people (real or not) through these simulations. Put another way, only the likenesses we build of other people, from details gathered in direct or indirect experience, allow us to know friends, historical figures and everybody else.

Why do we simulate others? Like everything minds do, this practice is functional. Here, the main function is understanding, in a special sense: these simulations give us the power to predict how people will act in new situations. Our ability to imagine conversations, to have an inner dialogue with people we know, is part of this ability. Say, for instance, you need a favor. Simulacra give you the power to plan this conversation. You can imagine different approaches to the request, then simulacrum responds to each. Because the simulacrum integrates everything you know about a person into the model, its predictions are going to be pretty good. The model also updates as you learn new things. As you come to know someone the predictions get better and better. These simulations help you make important social questions, such as can I trust this person? Writers should know that these simulations also lead to empathy. These mental models give us the opportunity to take others' perspective.

Humans Use the Exact Same Simulacra for Fictional Beings

You need to understand a bit about how simulacra work to write characters more effectively. Dare to dream, in this case literally. Dreams show how these mental models work. Science currently holds that dreaming originates in attempts to craft narratives from pseudo-random neurological activity. To put it in hopefully more accessible terms, your brain's sensory neurons keep firing while you sleep. These chaotic inputs could be flashes of images, for example. Then, they enter your brain's "higher" functions, which attempt to assign meaning by turning them into a story. Now, try to remember and retell a dream you've had. Due to the narrative you've crafted, your dream has story elements, world, plot and so on. It probably has characters. Whether they are people you know or horrible monsters, your dream has tapped into simulacra, one you already had or spun up during the dream. These dream characters sit at a kind of halfway point between real people and fictional characters. Our brains use the same mechanism to relate to every being on this spectrum.

To go a step further, consider how dream characters behave. Curiously, they seem to act independently despite clearly being our creations. Their capacity to seem independent emerges from their existence as simulacra. Put another way, the models your brain holds allow them to act as beings. Perhaps, you were chased. If so, your mind tries to explain; why were they chasing me? You turn to their simulacrum for answers. Though they're not real, you get an answer as you would for any being: they're hungry, mad or maybe want to return the cell phone I forgot. In other scenarios, the simulacrum's goals may cause the chase. Maybe you dreamed of a greedy dragon, they're going to want your gold. Here's the lesson: simulacra contribute to the story as ostensibly independent beings. Readers see them react to circumstances according to their own will because they're active simulations.

Here's the astonishing point to cherish: the simulations humans build for real people and fictional characters are fundamentally identical. Our brains build, store and interact with them in the same way. True, imaginary beings are "tagged" as fictional (otherwise, we wouldn't know they're not real); however, that doesn't change the nature of their simulations. The fact that they're not actual people is merely a bit of info enmeshed in the simulacra. Put simply, we know great fictional characters, like *Don Quixote*, as well as we know our friends and family. In fact, access to their thoughts — inner monologue — allows us to know them better than real people in many cases.

If you're dubious, consider anthropomorphization. This describes how we attribute human qualities to non-human entities. We talk to stuffed animals and similar "beings" with no ability to respond. (Apologies to these friends.) These conversations utilize the same mechanism talked about above when you thought through asking for a favor. We perceive these objects as genuine beings with dreams and goals, like us. To reiterate, we're also able to make solid predictions as to how they'll behave and act on them. Turning off the light, for instance, scares Teddy, so it's kind to warn him. It's hard to say whether this is a misuse of an evolved mental function or not; you can see it as "hijacking" for this reason.

Science shows that our brains have the ability to form simulacra from fiction; *publishable* characters depend on this power. Takeaway this key fact: to the extent your characters exist as beings, they do so as simulacra. The opposite also holds true: absent a simulacrum, readers won't perceive your character as a being. This equivalency — beingness equals a simulacrum's presence and vice versa — delivers a quick way to meet and check for a preliminary requirement: authenticity. Here it is. If a character has corresponding simulacrum in someone's brain, they're authentic; otherwise, they aren't. In this view authenticity is a clear-cut, binary necessity, either your character is or isn't. A simulacrum's existence is the sole deciding factor. To forcefully restate: it takes a corresponding simulacrum for your reader to perceive your character as a being. This makes understanding how simulacra form and develop absolutely critical to your success as an author. This guide is essentially devoted to this topic.

Authenticity and Simulacra

You're likely to have heard about the uncanny valley. Researchers find humans "get along" better with inanimate objects, such as robots, with human-like features. These features, ridiculous as they may sound, work. Specifically, we're more likely to say a bot with googly eyes is friendly, for instance. However, continuing to add features, trying to make the robot look more human, backfires. At some point, the human looking bot tips into a bot looking human, and its human counterparts pull back. It seems creepy at best and sometimes disgusting. Our species is very good at sniffing out this fakery. This quasi instinct makes the robot that comes closest to being human the worst of all (Commander Data is an exception). You can take the uncanny valley, the almost yet not human robot, to be a failure of authenticity, something humans don't accept as a fellow being. The uncanny valley poses a challenge for writers to meet that concerns authenticity. Loosely defined, authenticity (forming a simulacrum) means perceiving a human like being.

Fortunately, you don't face the same challenge as robot makers. Leaving aside the fact that words can't engender the same creepiness as a rubberized monstrosity, readers expect to accept your characters. They have that mental capacity standing by and ready to go. This means that prompting simulacra isn't hard; it takes very little to initiate the process. Your brain, which has practically unlimited storage capacity, holds countless simulacra. Everyone you've ever met or heard of exists in your mind as a simulacrum. Past that huge number , there's more; every being you've dreamed of or imagined also has a corresponding model. In short, your brain contains thousands of models. Adding one more isn't a big deal. In fact, simulacra pop up for anything that passes a very low threshold, generally a name is enough. What's in a name? Shakespeare's Juliet asks; the scientific answer is a simulacrum.

Meet Pat

How do simulacra work? Consider Pat — a friendly sort who will help us throughout this guide, for example. Say that name aloud: Pat. In speaking their name, what did your mind's eye see? There's Pat, a generic human, following the pattern set by your baseline. Now, let's add the smallest detail: the Firefighter. Bang. Now, Pat the Firefighter, depending on your firefighter notions, probably has a helmet. Maybe your Pat is at a station with a Dalmatian, sitting near a fire engine. Your mind requires no detail other than a name and label to complete this model; that's simulacra at work. In combination with the firefighter stereotype (which we'll discuss), this model emerged in milliseconds. Critically, even in this barebones formulation, Pat has the quality of beingness.

After the initial "spin up," the more you hear about Pat, the more detailed the simulacra becomes. Age and family, for instance, are automatically added — the technical word is "elaborated" — at their mention. For example, upon reading "Pat's family," the model instantly expands. Your Pat might now be older with three kids while other versions are young and single; a few might be retired, perhaps receiving monthly visits to hear stories and admire scars from heroic work. Notice that these simulacra are still complete; Pat remains a being. It's remarkable how easily you imagine all three Pats. From there, the permutations are endless. Humans are so good at simulacra that you can wield a few words as a magic wand to summon almost anything into beingness: Greek god, sapient mountain or talking fish. The possibilities are literally infinite. One famous character, Pinocchio, demonstrates this well. His narrative centers on a quest to become real, but readers, paradoxically, treat him as such from the start. By the end of its first part, he has the same, if not more, humanity as Geppetto.

Authenticity is Easy

By now, you should see how easy it is for a character to be authentic. According to our criterion, having a corresponding simulacrum is all it takes. This way of looking at authenticity also places emphasis on the reader. What matters is only how readers recreate your character in their brain. Remember that. It's up to the reader to evaluate the words you write; there are no substitutes. This means, for instance, any tests of your work, including the one for authenticity described shortly, should focus on assessing how your words impact readers — what they take away from your story. It also suggests adding copious details is not necessary, or even helpful, when it comes to making a character "believable." We'll return to this point.

Here's the authenticity bottom line: when well-formed simulated beings grow within your reader, they relate to them as any other being (with all the complexity it entails). If all goes well, the link between your characters and readers steadily develops as your story progresses, ideally reaching the grokking, deep empathy, we defined. On the other hand, with the wrong information, be it too little, too much or conflicting, derails this process and prevents simulacra from forming. If the simulation isn't properly launched, or if it falls apart later on, readers won't relate to your characters as being. Put another way, if words intended to prompt a simulacrum, to introduce a character, aren't presented well, no simulacra will form and may cause readers to abandon your novel.

All this said, don't worry too much about authenticity. This advice may seem to defy your intuition, besides much advice, but remember these two halves of this discussion. First, our brains are set up to accommodate social life. We regularly meet new people without fuss. Second, our brains can be coaxed into treating anything as a being, up to stuffed animals and kitchen appliances. As an author, all you have to do is not derail this natural process, the one that recreates other beings as simulacra. Humans are so focused on figuring out others — at least at first impression — you should stand aside and let our social natures take their course. Pat the firefighter shows how much a few seeds yield. We'll spend some time talking about choosing the right seeds. However, the real work begins after they germinate, when it comes time to grow the simulacrum into a character worthy of grokking.

Use Retelling to Collect Feedback

There's a quick and easy way to assess authenticity. Recall your character is authentic, given our discussion, as soon as the reader spins up their simulacrum. Pretty easy right? Indeed! You only have to check that your potential being's corresponding simulacra exists after reading. So, have someone read and then ask questions. Specifically, find a "beta" reader, a volunteer, and have them read the chapter (around 3000 words), which contains your character's introduction. Then, ask them to retell their reading in their own words. Don't interject once they start; let them talk. Only after they've run out of steam, ask them to describe the character if they haven't already. If they mentioned the character, feel free to ask probing questions covering the character's vital aspects. You're looking for a relatively enthusiastic and sufficiently complete description of your creation. Volunteers usually find this task fun, and far less taxing than the standard procedure, asking for comments. While being less onerous, this technique — perhaps surprisingly — produces more useful information.

Retelling's Advantage

This technique's utility stems from an alternative view on collecting feedback. Ideal evaluations are organic and spontaneous; this seems rather obvious. However, the common practice — asking for comments — is neither. Moreover, commenting doesn't speak directly to whether your writing fulfills its purpose; in this case, launching a simulacrum. Direct evaluation calls for effectively testing specific aspects of your writing's performance. Commenting, in contrast, has a different aim. It encourages beta readers to see themselves as partners, enlisted in your effort to create *publishable* characters. The retelling test encourages the opposite, experiencing your words as readers do. In this vein, the best reteller is a reader who loves your genre but knows nothing about the project at hand. Also, be wary of those with personal relationships. Friends, fellow writers and paid professionals, though well-intentioned, aren't as good as naive betas. Sometimes factors beyond the page — relationships, barter (you comment on my stuff, and I'll return the favor) or pay — influence their response. It's fine, of course, to have co-authors and helpful professionals; just don't use them for this guide's tests unless you literally can't find anyone else.

The need for spontaneity also makes it vital to ask for feedback soon and in the right way. The retelling prompt, in particular, encourages honest reactions and eliminates distance. Try to catch them right after they've finished reading. You'll gain the best results when you can see the reteller's face. Examining their reactions closely, but surreptitiously. This is not an interrogation; fixing them with your intense gaze under bright lights sets the wrong tone. The session should maximize your participant's ease; let them go at their own pace while you chill, observing indirectly and very discreetly. Your main job is to listen; think avuncular conversation, where the doting uncle delights at every word.

Remember the goal, to see whether your words have the desired effect. As they delight or stumble, you'll know what to keep and where to revise. If you see your respondents pause before answering, let alone saying that they don't know, you'll know your work requires revision. Try it once to see its efficacy. Many authors are surprised to learn their words do not have the intended effect. You may think you've made a great intro, but tests may show otherwise. Maybe the reader didn't recognize that your creation is a main character or missed central facts. On the other hand, successfully passing these inspections gives you confidence; you're on the right track.

Assess Authenticity with Retelling

In terms of authenticity, when their recounting includes your nascent character's basics, consistent with your intentions, you've succeeded. With authenticity confirmed, you're off to a great start. You've created a character who is perceived as a real being. On the other hand, if the reader struggles to remember the character or has little to say you're in trouble. When you see this, know your character needs work. For some reason, typically because you haven't spent enough words on them (spending too many words is covered below), there isn't enough material for your volunteer to recognize their beingness and form a simulacrum. Revise your character — add words, subtract them or reorganize the presentation — and test again. If you're having trouble, move to a last resort; put in a scene where a third being meets that proto character. The reader's mimicry of the third inevitably leads to a simulacrum, so you can see what passing this test looks like.

In sum, authenticity is vital but simple to achieve. A few details encapsulating an object's beingness — sometimes just a name — is enough to get the reader's mind to accept almost anything as a human-like character and respond accordingly. Remember, in the reader's mind, an authentic fictional character is no less real than their life partner or someone they meet at a party. Nevertheless, authenticity only opens the door to the deep linkage you're trying to nurture. In other words it's just a start. The hard part of writing *publishable* characters is harnessing authenticity's far more fickle cousin: investment.

Your Primary Challenge: Reader Investment

Romantic love is a convenient, yet unendingly mysterious, link that parallels the one we want your readers and characters to form. The operative expression "to know me is to love me" is empirically true; we tend to love those we know best. (Yes, it applies to villains.) This saying hints at your challenge since empathy comes from knowledge. Yet, this observation also hides a critical prerequisite. Getting to know someone takes time and, more importantly, attention. Without investment, love is superficial at best, nothing like true love we want. Romantic comedies demonstrate both slides of this "getting to know you" process. Cue the appropriate Rodgers and Hammerstein song. While one side falls in love at first sight, the would-be significant other has to notice and care enough to, for lack of a better word, investigate. Your reader is unlikely to fall into the first category and fall instantly in love. Thus, you must entice readers into paying attention and investigating before anything else.

Doubling down on romance bashing, getting to know another takes place in the brain not the heart; more precisely, to know a person, you model them in detail. The term, to get very technical, for adding detail to a simulacrum is elaboration. Here's an example. When talking about someone you barely know, you might say they're a nice person. A fully elaborated simulacrum, in contrast, might include an anecdote. They not only helped their friend move but also brought snacks to keep everyone energized. They stayed after everyone else left, though they had other plans, because the friend seemed unsettled. Meanwhile, they arranged the furniture and cleaned up; finally leaving after their housewarming gift, fresh plants, was delivered. These embellishments could go deeper. Grief stemming from their mother's death led them to overdo things, knowing deep down nothing could heal that wound. Phew! They really are a nice person, and we kind of understand them, too. See the difference elaboration makes?

When it comes to characters, reaching your goal — grokking, requires a fully elaborated simulacrum. If you were able to transfer your model of these beings directly from your mind to readers, like a mind meld, you wouldn't need this guide, but that's not the case. You must use words. Over your story's course, you have to carefully stream words, avoiding info dumps, in order to methodically build readers' simulacra to match yours. We're getting ahead of ourselves. Let's ignore these subtleties (for the moment) to focus on getting readers to attend to your character. You're familiar with these "meet cute" type moments, they mark the start of reader investment. We'll concentrate on what makes people interested in others, the push or pull governing whether readers will begin their journey toward grokking.

Though spinning up simulacra takes little effort — again, humans do it nearly automatically — new people are equally easy to ignore. This happens a lot. You meet someone, pigeonhole them and move on. Due to constant demands on our attention, it's our default. This makes fostering investment dramatically harder than establishing authenticity; you're swimming upstream. Your characters must, must, must attract their attention, particularly your protagonist. Sparking interest is the metaphorical turn to face and focus on the would-be character. Researchers have a lot to say about this spark: the factors that orient us toward a few strangers and away from the rest.

Attract Investment through Identity

Similarity is one route to attracting investment, but it's more complicated than making a copy of your potential fan (were that possible). Sociological researchers observe we tend to like people who are like us. You've heard "opposites attract;" overwhelming evidence contradicts this cliche. Instead, the right cliche is birds of a feather flock together. Put another way, relationship success generally correlates with how similar two individuals are. In ordinary life, as opposed to romantic fantasy (to be discussed), nearly everyone dismisses opposites immediately, if not sooner. Many say ingroup affinity and outgroup bias, which govern our reactions to new people, are hard wired reflexes. It sure seems that way. Humans seek affirmation and eschew confrontation; in lay terms, people like us make us more comfortable. Similarity, for instance, reduces awkwardness and social risk. You can test this. See whether you gravitate more toward people like you or not the next time you're in a group situation. No cheating.

That said, digging deeper into science offers some hope to authors by showing how to bridge the gap between dissimilar people. In short, Walt Whitman was right; we're multifaceted. You may be a parent, student, worker, child, sports fan, taxpayer, customer and nearly infinitely more all at the same time. For example, we can easily picture a mom with her own ailing mother, taking a break from working as a doctor and listening to a Yankee game while standing in line for coffee. There's five. Psychological studies suggest adults have an average of thirty available personas. Think of each as a potential identity, which comes to the fore in response to a situation. To mobilize these prospects, you need to understand the second half of the identity puzzle — our active identities reflect the situations we face. Your control of the citation turns these facets into resources. This notion unlocks the door to an initial sliver of attention.

Let's bring back Pat the firefighter to see how this process works. Despite the exposure's brevity, you already "know" Pat; your mind has a bundle of their details organized into a person model. Use inner dialogue to examine what comes to the fore as situations change. Like Pete Townshend, ask your Pat simulacra *"who are you?"* Of course they'll answer Pat, you may have invented a last name, too. This is kind of a default, without context providing a first name is the standard responsible. Now, put Pat in a particular situation. They're still Pat, but the context brings another chunk of identity to the fore, almost making them someone else. At a child's school, they're a parent; *I'm here to pick up my kid.* When on duty, they're a firefighter; *do you have something to report*, and so on. Their response — their active identity — changes to suit the circumstances. This same pattern governs your readers as well as your characters. Each has a multiplicity of identities available, from which context selects one for the reader.

Here's the key: interest sparks when your character's and reader's identities intersect. It's up to you to create commonality. It might seem easy to meet this challenge because there are so many possibilities, all of humanity's diversity. Flipping through the Comprehensive Character Developer (this guide's second part), also at https://bardsy.com/character, you'll find 73 specifics of a being, for instance. Further, readers are also predisposed toward making an initial investment; after all, they bought your book. The creative challenge is to set up a connection that also contributes to your novel. In watching Star Wars, for example, the potential hero within all of us responds to Luke Skywalker. In reading The Count Of Monte Christo, Edmond Dantès' actions are reasonable, i.e. in line with our own instincts for justice and revenge.

To structure your options regarding what commonality to emphasize, it's useful to place possible overlaps between your character and readers into two categories: character and situation. Basically, your impetus can put "normal" people in extraordinary situations, extraordinary people in "normal" situations or (most likely) blend the two. The quotes surrounding normal signify the following paradox: people tend to think they're normal while also thinking they're special. Few of us would readily admit to deviating from a human baseline, to being a weirdo to strangers. Meanwhile, everyone operates from a selfish perspective that makes them feel unique. We can't help it. Being trapped in our heads makes adopting others' viewpoints an arduous task. (We'll discuss this universal finding — Fundamental Attribution Error — in the final chapter.) The difficulty abandoning our ego presents is part of what makes fiction so captivating; it's somehow easier for us to identify with and connect to a story character than someone sitting next to us on a train.

Wait, there's more bad news. Like it or not, a large part of how humans see themselves revolves around what they aren't and, equally, who they hate. It only takes a slight push to awaken these divisions, which harden under attention. Division goes to bolstering — I'm smart; they're stupid — along with fear and anger. Politics shows how easily prejudice spirals trigger, particularly with impersonal others. This short diatribe is not meant to endorse misanthropy, rather it's intended to highlight how powerful our ego is relative to our concern for others. Don't spread hate; use this tendency, carefully, to gain investment.

Despite this kind of self-centeredness, certain universals might advance your quest for attention. Flaws illustrate one widespread feature of human life. You're familiar enough with the exhortation perfect characters are boring. Human insecurity has made this advice worthwhile since ancient Egypt. Still, flaws serve a more important purpose than making characters "real," which you now know is not difficult. Flaws' purpose lay in jumpstarting engagement. Who hasn't felt self-conscious or made prideful mistakes? These could serve as an overlap between character and reader. That said, flaws come in many flavors. So, which should you pick? This question gets back to the broader issue: aligning your characters and readers, which we'll cover under the heading picking the right seeds.

And, Attract Investment through Situation

Besides shared identity, your character's situation can also spark reader interest. To repeat: identity offers one route to mutuality, situations offer another. (You should aim for both.) Recall that readers seek to live vicariously, to enter the character's mind. Achieving this grokking also means, underline this thought, the reader has entered the story. Put another way, in route to grokking, readers will discover themselves facing the character's challenge. We can call this surrogacy. Contrary to what you may believe, situations have as good if not a better chance of winning empathy than shared identity. An effective setup entices us into extreme, wholly alien circumstances, like ET — lost and far from home. A strangely shaped greenish puppet elicits feelings your human characters would be lucky to match.

Situational sparks tend to arise from intrigue. Humans are curious beings (another important generality), and readers tend to be the most curious. Use this trait to your advantage. Naturally, curiosity ties to the search for meaning we discussed. It should be clear that readers' many facets come with a multitude of interests. Genre (mystery and romance, for example) does, however, limit the situations you can construct. To digress, it's best to think of genre as the expectations readers bring to your work. Above all, you must meet these expectations if not transcend them. With respect to sparking interest, these expectations rule out some scenarios and increase the likely reward from others. Consider horror; these fans overwhelmingly respond to a scare more strongly than anything else. This pattern also suggests you should be intimately versed in your potential fans' genre. If you're not, get busy.

It takes context to make a given situation alluring. With the right construction, almost any situation can seduce the reader into a character's metaphorical shoes. Some reactions are more reflexive. You wince along with a friend who's stubbed a toe. From the arts to athletics, spectators' feelings match participants'. Being limited to words puts writers at a disadvantage when it comes to reflexivity, an immediate physical empathy. To achieve the desired impact, your writing has to deliver roughly equivalent information to other media or as real life. This challenge can only be met by building your situations well. As Goldilocks would say, not too much or too little but just right. Relying on what readers bring to your work helps you achieve this balance. (We'll fully discuss this topic in this guide's next chapter under the "Co-Creation" heading). To preview, words have a power other media lacks.

Compared to readers, viewers have a harder time imaginatively stepping into a character's place. There's evidence to suggest that readers' simulacra end up being more detailed than those belonging to movie audiences. Fiction has another huge advantage in provoking intrigue. Nothing limits your creativity. In film, the biggest animated blockbusters can only do so much; they'll never top the scenes you and your readers co-create no matter how much money is spent on special effects. Some novels, in this respect, are "unfilmable" or have disastrous adaptations, for instance. It takes an almost miracle to bring these tales, nodding to you *Lord of the Rings*, to the screen.

Writing is the medium closest to pure imagination. You can push or push past anything you dream up. Let's mention one low hanging fruit: transgression, i.e. violating social norms. Transgressive acts hardly ever occur in public (by definition). Fiction's privacy, in contrast, opens doors that a vanishingly small number would ever actually enter. In your imagined world, however, anything goes. There are many aspects where you can push boundaries, not limited to scope, level of detail and outrageousness. These breaches, of course, are not necessarily about sex, either; the other six deadly sins, such as greed and wrath, all offer opportunities to grab your would be fan's attention.

Think of it this way: fiction invites the reader to leave themselves behind as they enter an alternative world, one you construct. You have the privilege to build anything readers imagine, fantasy or nightmare. Better yet, you can push past their notions in favor of your own. Your writing can deliver dreams and horrors beyond anything they've imagined, and you don't have to pay a film crew. As you're scheming, don't forget the aforementioned curiosity. Human minds love to play what if with their scenarios or yours. Don't go too far; instead, exercise a constrained creativity. Yes, that's a bit contradictory, but you're telling a story. You absolutely must maintain coherence, which among other demands, includes effectively contextualizing the characters you offer. Naturally, we'll discuss this further. To win love you also must pay attention to genre and taste. For some readers, going big is the best option — a multiverse exploding; for others, destroying a marriage has more impact than destroying planets. Know your audience to decide correctly (and test).

For an extra kick, use immediacy to enhance the effect. Maybe, you present an everyday but intense situation, like cars colliding or a kiss. It doesn't take a stunt team or intimacy coordinator for you to produce such scenes. Wish fulfillment presents an entirely different option; let readers join your character in the lottery winning moment or as they open the door into another planet. Everyone knows fiction isn't real, so trust your readers to go along. They will, provided you write the story well. Remember once they've taken that first step, adding additional details (elaborating) snowballs into amazing characters. You have everything to gain from getting them to take the plunge. And, these are just examples; in knowing your story and your reader, you can do way better.

Use Retelling to Assess Initial Investment

The retelling test for investment extends the one used for authenticity. So, follow the same instructions; use the same criteria to pick a volunteer: genre fan, knows little about you and especially your work. Because authenticity is so easy, it's ok to assess it and investment at the same time.

To test for investment, look past the simulacrum's presence. You want to see the volunteer elaborate on your details. This may seem weird; why would we want them to add things on their own? This question gets to the heart of "Co-Creation," which will be discussed in great detail. For now, realize readers can't help filling in details as they imagine your creations. Even if you didn't write about what your creature is wearing, for instance, readers' minds picture a fully-dressed being. So, readers fill in the gaps and give a character an appropriate outfit. This is how minds work, much like we're able to see misspelled words correctly. In terms of this test, these additions signal investment; the volunteer was paying attention.

For example, they added clothes. So, keep track of how you described your characters to see if the volunteer remembered the details and added any of their own.

In the interview after your first chapter, look for one or two additions to the details you provide that expand on their identity. Investment also appears in, for lack of a better word, emotion. Observe their talking speed, facial expressions and other nonverbal cues to assess the strength of their reaction to your character. You're not looking for a particular emotion, just some evidence of feeling indicating their interest. Strong emotion, for example, could be a broad smile, a muttered curse or a vigorous nod.

There's an additional requirement: your volunteer's embellishments must follow your lead. For example, they shouldn't add contradictory details. Putting a firefighter helmut on a doctor raises questions; it could be a huge red flag. The reader may not be seeing the character as you do. When this departure happens, the reader is literally experiencing a different story. Perhaps a tiny inconsistency won't have too much effect. On the other hand, these little errors can accumulate to disaster. Be aware of this problem while you look for good augmentations. Alternatively, look for good augmentations while being aware of this problem. It's very important to keep this in mind from your novel's testing's start to finish. You'll see evidence for ongoing investment appear in the form of volunteers rounding out your creations. Why is this vital? Because in co-creating, they — not you — bring your character to life. When they fail to expand on your writing, your character remains lifeless words.

Here's the best follow up to ask for testing investment: what advice would you give the character, or what would you have done in their situation? This question capitalizes on humans' irresistible urge to tell others what they would do. For example, good horror movies make you scream "look out" while game show viewers shout out answers. In friendly conversation, rare is the person who'd rather continue listening to problems than interrupt with a "do this." Watch them; they strain to keep their mouth shut and concentrate on what someone else is saying. Welcome this tendency to offer spontaneous advice because it serves your purpose.

In this part of the interview, give volunteers' urge to render opinions free reign. Again, you're not interested in what they think of your writing. Yes, it's extremely difficult to remain dispassionate, especially in the face of criticism. Silently repeat your goal, which is to collect information that will increase your odds of success. While resisting the urge to scream, calmly ask them to refrain from offering opinions on anything other than the character's choices until the end of the session (when they won't matter). At the moment, you want to evaluate the volunteer's ability to understand and empathize with your character's options. An invested reader will freely offer thoughts, insults or approval, not that they'll affect your fictional character. If you've achieved grokking, they'll accurately recount the choice and may endorse it: I would have done the same. By the same token, you should also welcome outbursts or lesser reactions because they indicate a substantial investment in the circumstances.

Remember high school English? The inciting incident is especially important. Not only does your first chapter introduce the main character, it also shares the choice that launches the story. Thus, the retelling should contain situational information about their choices as well as a decent prediction. The underlying logic is discussed in this guide's final chapter under the "Agency" heading. Again, you may have to probe to get these answers. Ask: what would you do in the same situation, or why did they choose what they chose? If they spontaneously expand on these predictions, so much the better; it shows major investment.

Respect the Test

One last thing: respect the test. If it shows your character isn't working, revise. In addition, know when to cut your losses if your creation doesn't catch on after several revisions. It's undeniably hard to accept failure and harder to act accordingly. Some would-be authors can't do it; they insist their writing doesn't need revision in the face of bad results. They rationalize failure with the classic: they don't get what I'm doing. Indeed. They don't get it. Who's at fault? Their "they" were potential fans; now they're gone. You can also opt not to test and produce novels to satisfy yourself. Maybe people will buy them, particularly if readers share your taste. On the other hand, to satisfy readers and sell books, you should write and revise for them. It seems clear enough. Then, test to gauge your progress and improve your storytelling.

Meanwhile, remember it's your story, testing merely helps you tell it effectively. Console yourself with the thought that changing or cutting a character isn't wasteful; it's a step on the road to perfection, a coherent story. When something's not working, think of it as permission to try something else. You may have to try several versions before finding a character who sticks and is worth building a novel around.

Two Big Dont's: Confusion and Boredom

Alongside the positives: authenticity and investability prerequisites, we need to add two things authors must avoid: confusion and boredom. To understand the nature of the damage these mistakes cause and how you can avoid them when writing your characters, we'll look first at a broader question and ask why do people read?

DNF (Did Not Finish) Is the Worst

Readers read for many reasons, which we can lump together as satisfaction. Satisfaction's causes are a shifting target. They vary from reader to reader and from one moment to the next. Typical motives include entertainment, education, escape, stimulation and connection. You can think of more. What's important is that knowing these desires helps you anticipate readers' reactions to your writing (as well as your marketing). Promotion, finding and getting readers to buy your book, falls outside this guide's scope. We'll presume the reader already has your novel, which narrows our focus to this challenge: to keep your reader reading.

Continuity in viewing or reading "content" has come to be the paramount measure of success. We may hate labeling our writing content, but that industry highlights this to be the best approach to measuring success. It sees success when viewers (or readers) keep going; in the same way those who stop represent failures — very simple and easy to measure. Netflix for example; they evaluate content by minutes watched and also track completion — whether a viewer drops a series before the end. Amazon, closer to home, pays Kindle authors by pages read. These practices' logic can't be denied. From a scientific standpoint, they're objective, either you start the next episode, turn the page or don't. Analysts take this to be a more reliable indicator than indirect reports like reviews or surveys. Observe how retelling shares these features insofar as it accesses recall, either you know the character or you don't.

In short, continued reading is the best indicator of an author's success. Put simply, an author's worst outcome is for a reader to stop reading. A potential fan's negative reaction overcomes humans' natural reluctance to abandon things; that's the ultimate thumbs down. Not finishing also carries dire financial implications. Money and effort spent on marketing evaporates. It could spread negative word of mouth: reviews and genre influencers loudly proclaiming how much your novel sucks.

Eliminate Confusion

So, how do you avoid this tragic outcome? Investigations, plus common sense, point to two causes of not finishing: confusion and boredom. Of these, confusion predominates. Think back on your own reading experiences. When novels spin out of control, it becomes hard to keep track of what's going on. It takes increasing commitment to keep going. Maybe you'll stick with Game of Thrones; lesser works don't have that attraction. Boredom is similar; page after page with little reward leads to diminished expectations for what's coming next. You can see flagging commitment when readers skip ahead, something Kindle tracks. Most importantly, everyone regularly takes breaks and stops reading — usually around 3000 words. The issue is will they return; conversely, what makes them hesitate?

On the positive side, the obvious answer is satisfaction; on the negative it's some kind of burden. Though you may not admit this aloud: publishing is a customer service industry. In serving your readers, avoid disorientation and tedium. Woe to authors who court confusion, it may be fun for them; for the reader, not so much. Consider the "mystery box" technique used in some media. The idea is to build a story on an ever more intricate puzzle while perpetually delaying any kind of resolution. Even in a master's hands, this gambit is unlikely to yield the kind of satisfaction necessary to win repeat customers. In short, a new take on screwing with readers has little chance to pay off.

Confusion (and possibly boredom) has its roots in incoherence; assuming you have a story to tell, this problem comes from a breakdown in transferring the story from your mind to the reader's. Recall, every part of a great novel contributes to its purpose — they're coherent. We'll specify coherence (and how to attain it) more precisely soon enough. For now, remember great novels are constructed to be meaningful. In mysteries, for example, reader satisfaction depends on meticulous setup. Aficionados judge authors who fall short of this standard harshly. Suffice to say, coherence and meaning go together; their presence banishes confusion and most boredom. So, we have an underlying priority, which is an antidote to those twin evils, to satisfy readers' compulsion to find meaning.

Recall how we're predisposed (as with dreams) to make sense of happenings by crafting explanations, i.e. narratives. Our endless speculations may or may not bear fruit in life — not so in well-crafted fiction; it rewards each and every investment. Should you spend pages describing how your character prepares their coffee, readers — usually subconsciously — will puzzle over the why. They unfailingly try to figure out why you spent your words on that scene. Of course, they do this to give meaning to the story their minds are recreating. Confusion occurs when readers can't add new information to their budding simulations. A red-headed character's hair may turn blonde, for instance. Elaboration comes to a screeching halt when the discrepancy is noticed. Did the newly blonde character use dye, are they alien chameleons or was the inconsistency a mistake? Absent immediate explanation, the reader's lost. The author forces them to choose between uneasily continuing, skipping ahead or giving up.

Deferring explanation doesn't resolve this dilemma. To illustrate, when a character does something unexpected, literally out of character, some authors defer providing an explanation. The reader asks what's going on, and the author tells them to wait, presumably offering an actual answer much later in the novel. For the author, who knows what's coming, that's perfectly reasonable. The reader, meanwhile, has no reason to trust the author. There's a problem because they're not mind readers. So, you may think "this is going to be so cool" while their reaction crosses from surprise to disorientation. Going from "wow, interesting" to "what the F is going on" begs the reader to give up.

Avoid Boredom, Too

Confusion's no less fatal cousin is boredom. Readers, somewhere in the back of their minds, continually wonder what's the point? Boredom can come from having no point or (much less likely) making the point too obvious. Steamy love scenes and ample gastronomic descriptions have their place. However, depending on the genre, even superb filler remains filler and can't be excused as "developing" characters. Detail without relevance invites DNF. Pay attention to the fact that most people give up between chapters. These breaks allow readers to assess their investment, usually subconsciously, and decide whether to continue. A thumbs down could manifest in procrastination or another failure to return.

In all, confusion and boredom are stumbling blocks, which need to be eliminated in order for the rest of your work to pay off. Eliminating these two obstacles clears the route to investment and empathy — that grokking where readers enter your characters' minds. Concentrate initially on getting the ball rolling by securing the first elaborations.

Chapter 04

Co-Creation: Embrace Your Readers as Junior Partners

PREVIEW:

1. You must accept readers as junior creative partners to bring your characters to life.

2. This reality means continually anticipating their reactions and leaving "blanks" for them to fill.

3. They fill these spaces with their cultural knowledge, chiefly stereotypes and archetypes.

4. Co-Creation requires knowing your audience and testing to prevent counterproductive contributions.

We know the ease with which readers spin up simulacra makes authenticity, the feeling your characters are beings, easy to establish. We also know that investment, the nurturing of simulacra which paves the road to grokking takes more work. Lots of work! The wonderful thing is you don't have to feed and care for these models by yourself, your readers will help.

Your audience's ability to fill in the blanks does much of the heavy lifting you need to nurture your creation. Going over their role is vital for this reason. These discussions will, first, help you appreciate readers' contributions, so you can plan for and take advantage of them. Recall how you must ensure your reader develops a character's simulacrum in a way that brings them to life and advances your story. Let's start with the obvious. Authors only have one tool in their kit, the words they deliver to the reader's brain. The pertinent question, then, is what effect do these words have? To recap, their primary effect is to establish and develop a corresponding mental model. However, your words are only one of the model's inputs. Readers often bring as much, if not more, to these models as writers.

Too often, writers see a division of labor separating them from readers, i.e. I write, you read. Great authors, in contrast, respect their readers by anticipating how readers recreate their characters. In this way, a novel's experience is really a Co-Creation, a result that joins the efforts of authors and readers. Success — finding adoring readers — depends on understanding and managing this process. To put it simply, you need to understand what reading entails to avoid failure, and this understanding will give you the power to forecast and test for your readers' contributions.

Co-Creation: How Writers Depend on Readers

Authors and readers are partners, particularly when compared to visual media's producers and audiences. Summarizing a great deal of research, reading qualitatively differs from viewing in this way: we react to movies — pretty simple. Reading, in contrast, defies generalization. Reading, at least, demands far more imagination. This fact is readily apparent. To be clear, the reader is very much the junior partner in this endeavor. As an author, you're your own production company; besides writing, you're the director, cinematographer and everyone else, usually including the production and marketing departments. Privileged are those with a supportive collaborator, agent or publisher. Your burden, however, doesn't diminish the reader's contribution.

Further, merely acknowledging you need readers is too vague. Of course, without their purchases you won't make money, and without their love you won't have a career. At the same time, it's equally unwise to write off criticism by saying "that's just one person." True, some people won't and will never love what you do (primarily due to genre), but you need readers all the same. Readers bring your story to life because your stories live in their minds. Further, it may not live in any mind if it doesn't live in one.

Co-Creation labels this lopsided interdependence. Naturally, a monumental effort goes into producing your polished manuscript. After that, however, the reader takes over. Their imagination does everything else, absolutely everything else, in terms of experiencing the novel. And, more importantly, each of them experiences it differently. Imagine yourself on a video call with every reader. Some sit at a desk, carefully dissecting each sentence while others skim your work on a noisy train. Moreover, they may have wonderful imaginations or be relatively dull. Further, they may do or be all these things at different times. While established authors tend toward more uniform audiences, your job is to please them all. No matter who they are and what they bring to the table, each deserves *publishable* characters and a compelling story. To deliver the goods, you need to understand and plan for their participation.

Thinking about architects and interior designers offers a good analogy. In collaborating to build a house, architecting the exterior takes precedence over interior details. The architect sets the space in which the designer works. A given room has dimensions, portals and maybe a dominating feature, such as a fireplace. The designer oversees what comes next. Like architects, authors can (and should) only do so much, leaving the rest to readers.

Imagine your story takes place in a Victorian library. Similar to Pat the firefighter, a brief direction — announcing the place — gets the reader's imagination moving. The reader visualizes bookshelves. Probably stuffed chairs, appropriate paintings and wall coverings appear — among the hundreds of details their image of a Victorian library includes. Do they imagine sconces, a rug or brass doorknobs? You won't know unless you test. Of course, testing everything isn't possible (nor necessary) so long as the reasonably expected embellishments align with your being. A poor owner might have a house layered in dust with tattered rugs, whereas a scientist's library would showcase exhibits tied to their specialty.

There's no end to the detail they could add, which is great as far as it goes. Naturally, you should see consistent details — those that align with your vision of the character — are truly productive. In our library example, the dust reinforced the owner's poverty while the scientific keepsakes spoke to their interests. In both, the reader enhanced the experience with complementary details, which advance the story.

Successful Co-Creation Harnesses Reader Knowledge

Co-Creation implies that you must, first, encourage the reader's imagination and, second, align it to your story. Alternatively, do your best to ensure readers add voluminous, appropriate detail. We'll expand on this mandate when we discuss stereotypes. Acting your need for readers, particularly their supportive embellishments, is a big step toward bringing your characters to life. Meanwhile, peril lurks. Incompatible elaborations will ruin your novel. For example, readers tend to locate scenes in the here and now; in the Victorian case, they'd have to remove the computer screens and air-conditioning ducts if they don't set the era correctly from the scene's start. The lack of the right seeds — or the right seeds in the wrong order — force readers to tear down and haphazardly rebuild their recreations to clear up their confusion.

Should you fail to manage readers, inaccurate embellishments will trip you up. One mistaken reader assumption might not be fatal. A critical misstep, however, can start an avalanche whose result will be two separate beings — a character in their minds that differs from the one in yours. To avoid this risk, we will work through an extended illustration, which covers how Co-Creation works. This sketch also introduces a critical psychological phenomenon, which you've undoubtedly heard of: stereotypes. You'll see how cultural knowledge accounts for a substantial portion of what readers bring to your characters.

Using Stereotypes Correctly

Stereotyping is another aspect of how people — your audience — relate to others. To understand it, and add to our foundational knowledge regarding characters, we turn again to science. We've tiptoed into this topic by discussing how easily we spin up different versions of Pat the firefighter. That example illustrates the challenge, as well. While we can marvel at our imagination's effortless conjuring (someone middle-aged, young or retired), a story's context makes at least two of these Pats mistakes. After all, a character can only have one age at a time. Naturally, what the reader infers about age must match what you have in mind.

Understanding stereotypes will help you nurture productive elaboration and avoid mismatches that risk the error avalanche. Though stereotypes certainly have bad consequences, authors must recognize their preeminence. Put simply, stereotyping is universal; these cultural artifacts pop up automatically and instantly in every human interaction studied. A stereotype, to simplify innumerable investigations, supplies additional information whenever an individual's group membership becomes apparent. So, a fire hose (pun intended) of associations intrudes whenever a membership becomes apparent.

Pat has shown this in action. Firefighters are the group and what sprang to mind (hats and so on) came through that conduit. Imagine a Halloween costume to see how stereotypes can benefit authors. Slapping on a cheap plastic helmet turns you into a firefighter. Better costumes add a badge, boots and maybe a Dalmatian. Like simulations, infinite detail could be added, making the costume ever more realistic. This reservoir of knowledge, embedded in the firefighter stereotype, sits like an untapped goldmine. Just three words: Pat, warehouse and inferno, can readily recreate a movie, like Backdraft, in their minds.

Stereotyping works by attaching information to a category. Technically, identifying someone's category, their group membership, triggers or "activates" a certain stereotype. Once activated, your reader accesses everything associated with the category and pulls in any seemingly pertinent information. This flood provides raw material for the embellishments readers add to your details. Your job is to set these triggers intentionally. At the same time, perhaps more importantly, you must eliminate inadvertent triggers. The more your cultural knowledge diverges from your readers, the more likely it is for unintentional triggers to crop up. For example, your characterization may unwittingly activate a stereotype that readers will find abhorrent. Less consequentially, you may bring in a nerd stereotype by leaving out a few words, for example "aviator sun" in front of glasses. The potential for miscues increases the need for testing, which assesses whether the reader recreates the being you have in mind.

Though the Pat example emphasizes visuals (mental images are part of stereotypes), readers' databases go past images, holding every imaginable nuance. Within this abundance are "softer" attributes, like traits, which are so important to authors. Firefighting and bravery goes hand in hand, for instance. Soft inferences are especially likely when it comes to archetypes, discussed shortly. These kinds of inferences play a vital part in, first, making your character real and, then, in setting reader expectations, which opens the door to subverting them in service of your story. Two words, "cowardly firefighter," come close to bringing a heart-wrenching picture to mind.

Potential Problems

Your lack of control over what stereotypes readers have can trip you up. In other words, everything floating around in readers' heads can influence their interpretation of your words. Part of the challenge comes from stereotypes' cultural and constantly changing nature. Most readers will distinguish retired firefighters from rookies, for instance. On the other hand, some people know enough about firefighting to separate big city firefighters from ones that work for the Forest Service. To them, they don't look (or presumably act) alike. For these readers, activating one when you mean the other is a problem. Others won't notice. Further, individual experience mutates these cultural concepts. This implies that cataloging every stereotype is impossible; there are too many to count. Further, they tend to overlap in inconsistent ways.

To use stereotyping effectively, recognize that your story's context plays a role in activating particular information floods. Besides being intentional when using group membership, the best general advice is to immerse yourself in your readers' subcultures by reading what they read, watching what they watch and following their social media (as best you can). Then, use your knowledge of these stereotypes when imagining and writing your character. And, of course, test! Use the procedures described above to see whether your volunteers are on track. In sum, stereotypes provide a vast reservoir of detail to use, but this wealth can make your job — getting readers to recreate your characters accurately — harder.

Archetypes

Archetypes are stereotypes' cousins because both rely on an activation to tap into a flood of background. Still, archetypes differ because they center on personality, not on group membership. Try this for yourself, to see an archetype as a member of a specific group. It's hard because they are so universal. Let's define personality; it's a set of consistent reactions that typify a being's approach to life. This definition shows how archetypes take their cue from paradigmatic simulacra, i.e. model individuals, in contrast to stereotypes, where individuality is more fuzzy. For example, the Greek god archetype brings to mind a being who is very powerful and probably beautiful despite possessing human qualities and flaws. Further, you can envision their behavior: vain and disdainful to mortals, quick-tempered and the like. It's not technically a stereotype because these features directly describe an individual, not a group.

For this reason, an archetype comes much closer to being a person than a stereotype. Hearing that someone, like Pat (our firefighter), is a warrior brings a more specific portrait to mind as opposed to saying some is Scottish, for example. As nearly complete people, archetypes hold tons of info: traits, interests, drives, values, self-concept, abilities and emotional patterns. It's a lot, and can be very useful. Remember, though, these are subtle qualities. For example, calling someone a "warrior" (or having the reader recognize them as such) doesn't necessarily mean someone is in an army; rather it suggests a host of expectations related to fighting at a deeper level. Perhaps this warrior has unusual discipline or they're headstrong but never duplicitous. That said, a similar flood of potential embellishment follows from archetypicalness. Archetypes tend to be tied more closely to storytelling while stereotypes crop up more generally in human interactions. It all comes back to psychology.

An archetypes' content is more stable, as well. We don't need to endorse Carl Jung's semi-mystical concept (Collective Unconscious) to see that they're cultural products. Put simply, these paradigms have been established and refined over millennia of storytelling. How many archetypes are there? It's an open question, but the leading answer is not too many. Lists of them, which are fun to make, run from as few as five to around thirty. After research and debate, we at Bardsy settled on seven: warrior, rebel, caregiver, castaway, tempter, mentor, wild card. Naturally, you know them well; if not, you need to bone up on your readers' cultural knowledge or find collaborators who can fill in this gap. We won't describe them here, save to illustrate specific points. The Comprehensive Character Developer incorporated these seven's details. Once again, it's at https://bardsy.com/character.

What makes archetypes special (and limits their number) is their functional role in stories. To see this, imagine a hardy band of seven adventurers, something Dungeons & Dragons enthusiasts can do quickly. The seven incorporate the archetypes listed above. Give them a challenge, perhaps a crazed monster blocks their path or something subtler. Each personality has a different approach to handling the situation. You can go through the list (warrior, rebel, caregiver, castaway, tempter, mentor, wild card) to readily make projections for each. The warrior bashes it, the temper seduces it, etc. This is what personalities do, respond differently. Archetypes extend this thought in that their approaches are distinctively unique. In other words, every human tendency boils down to these seven (or slightly more) types. It's amazing. You can try to imagine any way beings could respond that isn't covered by an archetype. If you can, it's easy to solve, add one more archetype.

In this way, archetypes' content encapsulates enormous wisdom about potential human behavior. Notice also how each archetype is a "pure" form. In the adventure party example, you only need seven (plus or minus) to cover every possible response. Does this mean there are only seven personalities? For our purposes, the answer is yes because having an eighth (or adding one more to what you have) leads to repetition. When you use archetypes, you take advantage of their repertoire of standard behaviors that automatically make sense to the reader. Further, using pure, powerful personalities is generative because there's always a strong reaction to your story's events.

As you'd expect there are pitfalls inherent to this resource. Archetypes tend to be boring and possibly counterproductive as pure forms. Readers have such a strong sense of an archetype's personality and this knowledge is so widely spread that they are cliched. Using an archetype without adapting it to your story's context, among other refinements, yields cardboard cutouts, which violate our authenticity prerequisite. The rare way to successfully use pure forms is as comic relief, like Captain America; they also work as foils, i.e. minor characters.

Application and Example

The takeaway is to use stereotypes and archetypes as building blocks, components of your characters. Deliberately sprinkling in their trigger works wonders. A few words can activate a reservoir of information. Moreover, this data comes from the reader, so it counts as embellishment and shows reader investment. This perspective reveals that great characters are hybrids, effectively combinations. We'll make a more precise claim in this regard in Chapter Six's coverage of description, which takes the form of Bardsy's Character Equation. To preview, this categorization directs you toward pulling aspects of your being's identity from three sources: you, cultural universals and distinctive aspects of people you know. For now, recall how the overriding authenticity requirement demands an individual distinctiveness, which many see as complexity. Judiciously mixing stereotypes and archetypes with parts of yourself and people you know helps surpass this threshold.

Let's finish the adventure party example to see how this mixing might work. Right away, you can see how having two pure warriors in a party would be duplicative and boring. Ways to fix this issue immediately spring to mind. Though reflexive, the form of these solutions sheds light on creating *publishable* characters. To cite one, imagine twin warriors; their identical reactions would add a nice humorous touch. Similarly, twin tricksters and their hijinks could be funny or extra evil. In these two cases, paradoxically, their twinedness makes neither pure. More prosaically, make one older and another younger; it's enough sand in the oyster to overcome the duplication. The insight is stereotypes and archetypes are an ingredient. From there, the best authors examine the infinite possible combinations and permutations to select the one that makes the story work

In sum, readers are your partners. While you do the heavy lifting, you need readers' contributions to bring your characters to life if only because your creations must live in their heads.

We're reaching the point where we can describe developing characters as a snowball, moving from your mind to theirs. The relatively few details you provide in your intro starts the ball downhill, steadily growing as you add words. The momentum, if you will, comes from tapping into the reader's knowledge and experiences. A large part of what they bring to your characters is organized into stereotypes and similar mental structures.

The unavoidable necessity Co-Creation presents makes testing absolutely essential. To be alarmist, pulling the wrong trigger can blow up in your face. You must think carefully about your character's details, and plan what stereotypes or archetypes readers will use to avoid this. Of course, we'll be covering adding detail in detail.

Thus, familiarize yourself with your audience's patterns of thought as best you can. Afterward, use the retelling procedure to assess what your words produced, both the attempted activations as well as inadvertent. Look through your volunteer's account to separate your details from their additions. If their embellishments don't enhance yours, there's a problem. Again, sometimes results are surprising. Try to figure out where their embellishments came from to help you "debug" their thinking. For example, tracing the origin of an embellishment to a specific archetype implies that other info from the source would be easy to tap. To perform this task, reexamine your words and probe the volunteer's descriptions to find the trigger. Likewise, idiosyncratic specifics, which are unique to a reader, may indicate resonance with one person but not anything generally useful. Overall, witnessing your volunteers' additions should make you proud; it means they've thrown their weight into your efforts and brought your co-created being to life.

Chapter 05

Coherence: Evaluate Your Characters in Context with the MCS and PI

PREVIEW:

1. Characters and story are interdependent, so your creatures must be evaluated in context.

2. Satisfying readers demands coherence, a synergy between characters, world, conflict, theme and plot.

3. You're an "auteur" and solely responsible for coherence.

4. Saying your MCS — a short, yet complete, version of your story — maintains coherence as you write.

5. Bardsy's PI is a comprehensive 23-item checklist that identifies issues preventing satisfaction.

We've established three foundational points with respect to *publishable* characters thus far. First, they're important (duh!). Second, while readers easily begin recreating your fictional beings, getting them to continually invest in expanding these recreations is much harder. And, third, their investment appears in the form of elaboration and embellishment. Then, and most importantly, their additions to these recreations of your characters (yes, it's a mouthful) brings them to life and fosters the deep empathy we call grokking.

This guide needs a final piece to complete its foundation, specifically it concerns how characters function within stories. This topic revolves around the fact that characters can't exist without stories and vice versa. This self-evident truth's implications are what's at stake: your creations must be evaluated in context. Often, authors fail to do this. They think about their characters in isolation, which leads to missteps. For example, they provide too much and / or unnecessary detail. These irrelevancies hurt the story. Somewhat counterintuitively, less is more when it comes to planting the seeds your readers need.

Maintaining coherence adds a third major goal to your to-do list; it's an imperative which binds character to the rest of a novel's elements. Be careful to interpret this sense of coherence correctly. Here, it doesn't pertain to characters themselves (though they should be coherent in a different sense, which we'll call integrated); it refers to your story as a whole. Thus, on top of creating authentic characters and winning ongoing reader investment, you must step back and think about your story holistically and the function your characters perform therein. This third goal — coherence — overarches the others and is the one, distinguishing feature of great storytelling. Put simply, it absorbs the two character goals: authenticity and investment. For example, focusing on coherence dictates when and how much detail you should deliver for each character.

We've referenced coherence several times already because it's so important. Do you remember Bardsy's definition of a story? It's a coherent combination of five elements: character, world, conflict, theme and plot. Coherence sits front and center in this definition, signifying its indispensability. Absent coherence, writing is mush, a set of words which doesn't achieve storyhood (or storyness if you prefer). To be crystal clear: the phrase "incoherent story" is an oxymoron. There are degrees of coherence, of course, which we'll talk about. For now, know that there's a huge gap between coherent writing and its lesser cousins. Moreover, it only takes a few missteps to destroy a story's magic. If this sounds overdramatic, reflect back on the confusion discussion, particularly the error avalanche threat.

Because coherence is so important, you must regularly evaluate how well you're achieving it. This task calls for tools, so this chapter's end offers not one but two. They help you pinpoint where your story works and where it falls short, so your revisions are productive and lead to a happier reader. First, we'll introduce the Minimum Complete Story or MCS. This tool serves as a handy compass and rough yardstick (or meterstick depending on geography), guiding your writing even as it evaluates how well your story's elements fit together. Next, we'll go over Bardsy's Publishability Index™ or PI. This tool, really a super checklist, digs deep into your novel and its parts to see whether or not they deliver good or great storytelling. Take comfort in its 23 dimensions, which cover all aspects of a story to provide precise, yet comprehensive, feedback. Use the PI checklist over and over until your story is perfected, as we'll discuss. Both of these instruments help analyze your characters in context.

Coherence and Reader Satisfaction are Near Synonyms

List some great stories (or personal favorites). Now, try to retell them. You can do it, and do it readily. It's astonishing how quickly they spring to mind, whole and ready to share. Be it Romeo and Juilet, Star Wars or The Count of Monte Christo your brain has each narrative at hand long after your last reading. In simple terms, great stories stick while lesser ones rapidly fade away. Where does this observation lead? Pragmatically, the link between great stories and memory drives much of our testing strategy — retelling, for instance. It also raises provocative questions, like why do we remember great stories so well? Of course, this leads to more questions: why do we love great stories so much? And, relatedly, why do readers pay for them? (That one seems quite interesting, right?) Exhaustive answers could fill volumes. Let's sketch one to suit this guide's purpose.

Why Are Stories So Long?

Stories obviously involve communication, i.e. sending thematic messages, yet some take a million words (Proust's In *Search of Lost Time* has 1.2). This observation prompts a question: why spend so many words on an apparently simple lesson? In other words, what happens when we tell stories as opposed to merely stating a message? Take The Count of Monte Christo. You could say something like this short paragraph in place of the novel. This guy, Edmond, was unjustly imprisoned and sought vengeance. Afterward, he'd tell you revenge is motivating and fun but not ultimately worthwhile. Yes, we'd need more space to cover everything Alexandre Dumas says; still, even a thorough lesson plan — stripped of every "inessential" detail — couldn't take more than a few pages. Compare that abridged approach to reading the whole thing, pitting half a million words against a few pages. In terms of energy spent writing and reading, it's an enormous difference. We must be getting an awful lot from those extra words.

There's a simple answer for our purpose, which captures the extra words' payoff. Readers demand them, hundreds of thousands in this case, because they engender deep empathy. Shorter messages, in contrast, can't provide an equivalent experience. Great novels use their length to establish characters' authenticity and earn continuous investment. As we'll cover, the extra words also set up the context and choices necessary for a rewarding vicarious experience. In this way, your whole story works synergistically to create satisfaction, deliver an impactful theme and win readers' love.

Look at any great novel, like Dumas'. He builds a world, an imaginary 19th century France, which readers can inhabit. He populates this setting with characters that surpass the thresholds we've set. The deep empathy his creations foster lets readers experience the chain of events, including the ever compounding internal and external conflicts. Finally, he weaves the story's themes through the plot's rise, peak and resolution. All five elements worked together to enmesh the reader; and then land a devastating punch (with the elusive wow) and promote greater understanding.

Our Brains' Story Template

The memorability of great stories, simultaneously, suggests our brains have a generic story template. This concept has caught some scientific and popular interest because it helps us think about stories and storytelling. Some, for example, argue our minds are "geared" for stories. This perspective suggests the mind's machinery makes remembering coherent narratives almost effortless. This intriguing theory, however, isn't backed up by a rigorous scientific description of said template. The problem is existing research methods can't map complex mental structures. In other words, we can't look into peoples' brains to see exactly how they remember stories. Possibly, this gap will be filled when researchers develop better technology. That said, assuming it exists, a universal story template leads us to very useful insights.

The idea that there's a preset mental pattern for all stories makes sense. Whenever you encounter a story, your brain appears to fit it into a metaphorical story-shaped box. Once filled, these packages are stored for future use. The fitting-into-a-box process also helps us appreciate the story. Dreams illustrate how this template works. Recall dreaming depends on attempts to create narrative to fill in gaps; these gaps must come from a pattern common to all stories. Authors should find thinking in terms of this template very useful. For instance, it suggests coherent stories are more memorable because they do a better job filling the template.

Achieving Coherence

Due to their length, novels do more to reveal human psychology than simpler messages can hope to match. They offer profound understandings, ones other formulations, or ones with fewer words, can't. Yet, length alone is not enough; you have to tell a story. You must effectively orchestrate its five elements (recall: character, world, conflict, theme and plot), so they fit together and synergize. This reasoning stands behind the claim that you can't analyze characters in isolation. You need context for grokking to arise, for instance.

How do you write coherent novels? It's not easy (an understatement). You'd be wise, nonetheless, to see coherence as your foremost writing goal. This aim pushes you toward great stories and satisfied readers. Writing for coherence means assessing your words, from sentence to chapter, from the bottom up. Likewise, it calls for writing and revising the entire novel, holistically, from top down. Keeping the micro and macro simultaneously in mind presents a real challenge. Why? Because the big picture changes as you write. For example, you get a brilliant idea; of course you add it in. Yet, it shifts the story. Bardsy's tools help you manage changes like this. The idea is to keep the top, the big picture, aligned with the bottom, the words you write. They work by making issues — large and small — apparent, so they can be effectively addressed. The payoff is intuitive, matching your words to the top down view of your story guarantees coherence

When it comes to *publishable* characters, the route to coherence proceeds in three stages which follow the writing to reading path. First, characters appear in your head, crystallizing as your story develops. Then, you have to calibrate (or recalibrate) your writing to ensure your readers steadily develop a simulacra for each. Finally, their recreations must reflect your vision, i.e. readers know your characters as you do. Accomplishing these three tasks — within your story's context — is synonymous with creating great characters, ones that readers come to know, love and remember.

Coherence and Story Length

Though these three stages are analytically separate, they overlap in nearly all authors' writing process. This is a good practice to adopt. It, crucially, means that writing coherent novels calls for a kind of juggling. Why? To deal with novels' length. Let's explain. Shorter stories fit your head, what scientists call your active memory. They can generally be written or told from memory in one metaphoric breath. (Of course, they require revision.) Indeed, the primary tool we'll use to promote coherence, the Minimum Complete Story or MCS, takes advantage of this capability.

When it comes to characters, shorter forms benefit from your ability to work from a more stable simulacrum. In other words, your creation has less opportunity to change while you write and even less when you tell the story aloud. (This doesn't say that your character won't change, crystallize or otherwise evolve between sessions.) You can't help making adjustments to improve your story. Still, your ability to roughly keep everything in mind as you type away allows you to more or less automatically reconfigure the rest of the story in response to any alteration your creations undergo.

In short, it takes little conscious management, i.e. process awareness, to keep a short story's balls in the air.

As story length increases, more effort has to be devoted to overhead. By the time you reach novel length, organizing everything so pieces synergize — to maintain coherence — has become a second job. It takes mindful supervision, besides writing itself, to produce a good novel. Thus, novel writing calls for a workflow that combines top down and bottom up approaches. Experienced authors know (and novices suspect) these obligations: you must write from the novel's perspective as you work on every individual paragraph and section. Meanwhile, you may have to stop in the midst of pounding away in the middle to update previous portions or your outline. Then, perhaps the most often ignored task, you have to make sure each chapter stands on its own, having a satisfying end which also lures readers into what comes next. As if that weren't enough, your first draft is only a milestone, requiring revision (often many rounds) to produce a polished manuscript. Phew!

Incoherence Equals Failure

Let's refer back to incoherence's consequences to build motivation for this monumental task. We covered one fatal result: confusion. This less than appetizing reader experience stems from a breakdown in the second stage: ensuring readers can steadily build simulacra. Recall the choice a hair color inconsistency forces. Upon noticing a red-headed character turn blonde, elaboration comes to a halt. The reader can stop to figure out what's going on, uneasily continue or give up.

Other symptoms of incoherence are more subtle but no less problematic. To be dramatic: neglecting coherence foreshadows doom (insert drums). A first slice at story coherence, with respect to your characters, concerns providing the right level of detail. As you know, too much or too little spoils the porridge. Authors usually provide too much. This issue continually crops up due in part to the prevailing advice concerning backstory. We'll discuss the proper use of backstory later; for now, the coherence teaches us to avoid overuse.

Consider this dicta to illustrate: start creating your characters with a sketch, basically a biography. Said bio's recommended length varies; one person actually advises going long and exhaustively listing every practicable detail (yes, it's nuts); others recommend a page or three. You should recognize that the longer these sketches get, the more damage they do. First, this practice encourages you to jam in irrelevant content. Novice authors often introduce these facts, aka infodumps, upon a character's introduction. These dumps, large or small, are largely irrelevant. While you have to describe your beings; this description only has to compensate for readers' inability to see and hear them — no more. Past some point, moreover, extra info is counterproductive. Do you expect strangers to run down their history? Of course not. However, the bio's existence constantly tempts you to add words. Perhaps your character isn't working, so why not throw in another paragraph? The reason, of course, is that substance matters more than length, so more will make things worse. The solution lay is to figure out the right words — to be continued.

Learning how the extensive backstory practice originated in theater may stiffen your resolve. Stage actors learn to flesh out their portrayals by crafting long, detailed and — above all — specific backstories. The actor prepares, right? (Google!) Acting is not writing. In contrast to reading, viewing demands little description. Likewise, viewing harnesses humans' innate ability to identify emotions. Directors use closeups frequently for a good reason: they trigger sympathetic responses (recall mirror neurons?). Thus, a scene's success hinges on minutia; a raised eyebrow, for instance, can be transformative. Meanwhile, the wrong expression derails the story. Much of backstory's benefit appears in helping performers control involuntary "micro expressions," which viewers are so good at catching. Espionage enthusiasts will recognize a parallel need for backstory in developing a spy's cover. The mission requires becoming another person, and fate rests on this identity standing up to brutal interrogation.

In short, meeting the authenticity standard we discussed replaces lengthy backstory on your way to writing a coherent story. Then, you must hold this authentic being in mind as you orchestrate productive reader elaborations. This guide's next chapter covers a faster and more effective way to bring your characters to life. For now: take this discussion of backstory to heart and reaffirm your commitment to weed out what readers don't need to coherently deliver the rest. Through these steps as well as using the tools described below everything in your novel will be relevant.

Auteurship and Coherence

Thinking about auteurship (yes, it's a word) completes our discussion of character, context and coherence — three Cs that go great together. This artsy term opens the door to the positive side of your responsibility to readers. An auteur is defined as the singular mind whose vision is responsible for any work of art. Let's follow this trail. André Bazin fathered this idea in late 1940s French film criticism. His problem was clear. France's literati dismissed movies as the product of the Hollywood system, studies, producers, etc. Such crass commercial produce didn't warrant serious cultural attention. Bazin, presumably a movie lover who wanted to get paid, proposed that movies qualify as art — and are attention worthy — because they come from the director's vision. To him, producers, craftspeople and the like, merely assist the director in the same way a sculptor's assistant prepares marble. Taking the director to be a singular creative force conveniently transforms film into art, so Bazin got paid. For us, auteurship teaches a lesson: art pieces are coherent works, which emerge from one human's vision. In short, there's causality: it takes one mind to create art.

You may see where this is headed: you're the mind responsible for your work's coherence. On the bright side, as an auteur, all credit for your novel's success belongs to you. Auteurship has a more immediate aspect than eventual fame and fortune, namely to ground your efforts to produce a coherent work. You can't abdicate that responsibility. Though readers are your junior partners, the buck stops (and, if all goes well, ends up) with you. The rest of this guide presumes you're a one person production company. In the attempt to create *publishable* characters, you get to be the director, cinematographer and everything else.

Hence, auteuring your story goes hand in hand with creating *publishable* characters.

Minimum Complete Story: A Big Picture Test for Coherence that Guides Your Writing

To help you produce a coherent story, let's introduce a basic tool: the Minimum Complete Story or MCS. As the name implies, it's the smallest, complete version of your story you're able to tell. The key point is the length, though short, it's still a story. It fits our definition: a coherent combination of five elements. Notice how this formula doesn't mention length. This absence reflects a fundamental fact; a story's word count is almost arbitrary. This property is called isomorphism, a mathematical concept where features remain similar as size changes. Let's use Abraham Lincon to illustrate isomorphism workings. Amazon offers thousands of books about him. One of the shortest, a children's picture book for kids, has about 250 words (pay attention to this length), while the longest seems to be a ten-volume biography, which has over a million. Yet, the core log cabin, Civil War president, assassination life story remains throughout. For fiction, consider the Count of Monte Christo; across translations, movies and abridgments, the tale (by and large) remains the same.

Isomorphism powers the MCS. Though it's a very short story; it's the same story as your novel. In other words, it captures your novel's five elements and the relations between them. You'll use it as a diagram or a satellite photo to guide and check your work. Meanwhile, compressing your story into the smallest space distills your story to its essentials. Besides raising the profile of what's important, minimizing your MCS makes it easier to keep it in mind, which means you'll be able to use it more effectively.

This tool applies the link between great story and memory in many ways. By loading your whole story in memory, the MCS serves as both compass and ruler. The compass part points your writing toward coherence while the ruler part helps you assess your progress in that direction. With the MCS, you can go back and forth between micro and macro as you write, regularly changing the order of, dropping, or adding sections even as you continually juggle your characters, world, conflict, theme, and plot. It supports your effort to orchestrate every part of your novel, including your characters, into a coherent whole. With practice, it minimizes the time it takes to get there, too. More importantly, using the MCS offers the optimal way to make sure everything you add about your character is properly contextualized.

The MCS helps you keep your story's elements in the air even as you reconfigure their pattern to maintain coherence. Stories, again for most, invariably change as you write. Inspiration hits at the most inconvenient times; you're in the shower when a way to improve your tale hits. Maybe this insight causes you to reshape a character or refine the conflict. That's great! Nine times or more, out of ten these changes are worth exploring. You rush to the keyboard and start typing. Now what? Every other aspect of the story must adjust to accommodate the change. Of course bigger changes require more adjustments. If, for instance, you change hair color, you could probably get away with a global search and replace. In contrast, if you alter your creation's parental relationship, every scene might need revision. For this reason, step by step plans and novel "templates" won't do; you need a dynamic approach to writing. You need to know how to: first, get started; second, make continued progress; and third, know when you're done. Yes, it still sounds linear; however, concentrate on the middle part; it's the toughest. How do you make progress as your story changes?

The MCS provides an answer, a technique which helps you cognize and reflect on your whole story as you write. Because you keep it in active memory, the MCS reflexively adjusts to reflect your story's growth, even as it shapes your writing. It links the big picture and the details, the macro and micro. In doing so, it creates a feedback loop that makes you aware of any major change's consequences. Then, should something shift, you can either update your MCS or revise your writing. So long as you do one or the other, you'll be ok. Keeping the MCS in rough equilibrium with your writing supports steady progress. On the other hand, trouble arises when your MCS and writing diverge. Should they get too far out of whack, you'll need to stop and do some rethinking. Best of all, as your MCS and your writing co-evolve, the correspondence between them ensures that your novel will remain coherent.

Creating Your MCS

To create your MCS, start with the main characters, then add the world. Remember to keep it short, no more than a sentence for each. (The gossip test presented below helps.) Plot comes in the form of an inciting incident, peak, and resolution, at most three more sentences. Now, tie everything together by telling these sentences as a story. When you're done, the conflict and theme should be crystal clear to you as well as any audience. Don't stress! Your first MCS version won't match the last. Moreover, give yourself permission to do a bad job on your first attempt. A new project's MCS can be almost crappy, up to vague descriptions and a missing peak or end. You should expect this and not let it keep you from using the tool. On the bright side, just trying to do one helps fill and refine your story's parts. Above all, your MCS can and should change; most authors can't do a full version until they're a third of the way into a first draft. On the whole, telling your entire MCS aloud from memory — it's vital — should take less than two minutes.

Use fairy-tale cues if you're stuck: once upon a time, then one day, unbeknownst and so on. Though seemingly trite, these introductory phrases are closely associated with the generic story template idea. Generations have used these for exactly this purpose. Don't be embarrassed; they really work. If you find yourself droning on listing each plot point, use a timer. You won't reach a fully distilled form before many, many repetitions. For practice, build an MCS for your favorite movie or novel, stripping it to the essentials while leaving the narrative intact. You'll see how quickly you can build their MCS to retell the story. After all, they're great stories; coherence lets you access and distill these tales even after many years.

Here's a very short Romeo and Juliet. Once in Renaissance Italy, Romeo, a headstrong teen, falls hopelessly in love with Juliet. But their families are rivals, worn enemies. As romance unfolds, friends and cousins kill. They weary of the conflict, commit to love and craft a plan. Mistakes lead to suicides, leaving families to mourn.

Notice how this example isn't a chronology, listing events. Also, your MCS shouldn't tease, like flap copy, nor include any editorial comments. Above all, keep it short, about 250 words — the same length as the shortest Abraham Lincoln. Coincidence? Maybe not. No matter what, never forget the goal: a stand-alone story, your narrative in its least possible form.

Using Your MCS

With the MCS tool, writing becomes a back and forth process. Keep it figuratively close while you write, pausing periodically or when needed to tell it aloud. Rehearsing your MCS, for instance, before you sit down to work sparks your writing and promotes efficiency. It may dispel writer's block, as well. (Miracle!) Most importantly, integrating the MCS into your standard operating procedure unerringly detects major story issues. Finding yourself or a volunteer confused during its telling screams some area needs more effort. Usually, this confusion stems from one element, like a character, changing; it can also point to other areas that need catching up after a change occurs. Again, your MCS may be incomplete at first, and it will change as you write and rethink your story.

Telling your MCS to others, perhaps in a Bardsy workshop, invariably helps. Oral storytelling, ideally to another human, engages your so-called story instinct. That brain "module" — a generic story template — works below consciousness to place narrative elements in their proper relation and also identifies what's crucial and what's not. Let your audience ask questions; their narrative sense will augment yours. When any listener smiles or nods you'll know you're on the right track. You'll know your MCS is ready when you or your beta listeners ask for elaboration, e.g. tell me more, instead of about essentials, e.g. hows or whys which indicate confusion and / or incompleteness.

Keep rehearsing your MCS until it becomes second nature and fixed. It's valuable to make each telling more precise and more dramatic. In addition, carefully track the length as your story develops. It may start around six or seven minutes but the final version should take under two. Longer than this prevents you from keeping the entire narrative in mind. As a bonus, you'll spontaneously generate ideas during these rehearsals, which will improve the work.

You'll have to say your MCS dozens of times (if not more) before it stabilizes. There's a huge payoff: when your final MCS mirrors your novel's 85,000 or so words it's broadly coherent. That's a huge accomplishment! It also means you're ready for the next test: checking your draft with our Publishability Index™. In "teaching" to this test, we'll also lay the groundwork for a plan to create *publishable* characters.

Bardsy's Publishability Index™: A Checklist to Analyze Your Drafts and Chapters Deeply

When your novel's first draft, subsequent drafts and sometimes chapters are done, you'll need another tool to drill deeper than the MCS in order to provide a more precise yet equally comprehensive examination. This tool, Bardsy's Publishability Index™ or PI, meets this need by listing every issue which prevents happy reading. Yes, it's quite a claim. If you're skeptical, take a look before you move on. An interactive version is available here: bardsy.com/stories/pub-index.

The PI answers questions that weigh heavily on every writer's mind. How good is my story? How can I make it better? Is it *publishable*? You know answers to these come in the form of accurate feedback. We've already discussed some ways to get it. When it comes to novel-length works, however, examining each portion gets tougher. Worse, the need to track how your story's parts come together exacerbates this difficulty. While the retelling method offers a potent way to investigate these issues, it's impossible (or at least inefficient) to check everything at each stage. Other approaches, like asking for comments, are even worse if only because they depend on the evaluator's attention and predilections. For example, reviewing an 85,000 word draft takes ample time and focus. Beyond stamina, whether you pay for it or not, what they happen to notice or miss is extremely important. This is where the PI comes in.

Everyone will tell you revision is the most important part of producing a novel. Revising iteratively, i.e. repeatedly using the PI as a checklist to detect and fix the biggest problem — then repeating — accommodates the steps necessary to keep cohesion. To explain, skill or luck may lead to a problem-free first draft. On a smaller scale, it's also possible to find a problem and address it in a way that doesn't affect the rest of your draft. Don't count on either. Further, you may wish yourself into believing you've caught everything. Don't bet on it. Be honest. Have an open, dispassionate mind and put yourself in your reader's shoes. It's the only certain way to success.

Why Does the PI Work?

Think of the PI as a checklist of story must haves. Should your story miss a check on one of its 23 dimensions, you'll know to focus your revisions there. We'll pay particular attention to the three PI dimensions that address character soon enough. Before naming them (and to generate some suspense as to what it says about *publishable* characters), let's go over its use. The idea is to apply the PI to successive drafts. With each pass you'll identify your story's most pressing issue. Then you "fix" it while maintaining coherence (that's job #1) until none remain. Hence the PI's name: a story with no issues is eminently *publishable*.

To bang on the importance of repeated revision or iteration, imagine you solicit and receive voluminous comments. The need to adjust everything after each change, as mentioned, implies you can only tackle them one issue at a time. Thus, every time you conduct a total review, you also need to prioritize your list of problems. Why? Because each change ripples throughout your draft. Minor issues, of course, can be fixed without a total rewrite. Major revisions, however, annoyingly and unfailingly impact multiple sections and several of your story's five elements. So, while the degree of necessary realignment differs, every change demands other modifications to prevent your work from becoming incoherent. Further, you should see that after fixing something major, your list of problems is outdated. Fixing one problem may have caused others, so you need to take another pass, create a new list and prioritize. You should hope a different, smaller issue appears at the top. Only repeated, top down revision guarantees success.

What makes the PI work is an open secret: it's a prescription, almost a recipe, for what makes a story good or great. Can there be such a thing? Absolutely. Everybody, including you, has some implicit idea as to what a satisfying novel looks like. This theory shows up every time one is read, either vaguely (the DNF thumbs down) or more definitively, like a favorable review. This is a great thing for you. When a novel meets a reader's personal standard for greatness, they love it. Their standard basically sets your threshold for victory, including word of mouth, repeat customers and all the other goodies authors adore. By the same token, readers won't love everything. Most of the time they finish a book, nod appreciatively and move on; sometimes, sadly, they don't finish. All in all, their personal theories split their readings into three categories: great, good and not.

When you ask for comments, a similar thing happens. The beta reader's idea of a good story stands behind the comments they make to you. Experts have a theory about what a great story looks like, too. They can't help it. People who teach writing or do reviews, for instance, must be able to communicate what makes writing better or worse to do their job. Imagine the caricatured Iowa workshop leader. This éminence grise belittles the participants, of course; nevertheless, they have some ideal story in mind that they bludgeon their protegees' drafts to match. Over time, their expert thoughts turn into a prescription for storytelling, so they can provide advice on call. Thus, a standard for what's good and bad in terms of any novel, i.e. a theory covering what makes a novel (or character) great, permeates these activities.

Bardsy's PI attempts to make our implicit theories regarding great storytelling explicit. It grew by gathering and organizing available advice on storytelling into a comprehensive list. We then dedicated much effort into revising and testing each item to ensure clarity. Some would say this task is foolhardy. They might say every story is unique, a subjective experience which defies systematic evaluation. This premise has some truth; however, it obscures what's possible. We can acknowledge stories are unique and feedback is ultimately an individual's opinion. Nevertheless, we can apply proven scientific techniques to account for this uniqueness and subjectivity. Teachers know these techniques regularly produce feedback that is at once individualized, yet systematic. They can help do the same for any story.

Finding Useful Feedback

Specifically, good feedback must satisfy three criteria:

First, precision. Imprecise feedback, such as that provided by a friend (or professional) who pats you on the back and says "great story," isn't helpful. Though well-intentioned, such comments are dead ends. The best feedback points to what works in a draft story and what doesn't. Further, it also sets a clear threshold for "working," which is intelligible to everyone using the standard.

Second, comprehensiveness. The best writing feedback must eventually answer the "how good is my story" question. This requirement demands a complete evaluation: one that addresses every aspect of a work. A long critique focusing on characters can be useful, but obviously leaves out much of what makes stories great. Worse from this guide's perspective, it may miss assessing how well these characters work in context.

Third, consistency. This may not seem so important, but put it this way: it would be nice for your writing to receive the same feedback no matter when it's read. Likewise, it's better if the feedback is similar no matter who reads it. Inconsistent feedback, in contrast, is not good. You'd have zero confidence in someone who offers one opinion in the morning and a different one in the afternoon. Similarly, a writing workshop which reaches consensus offers more direction, all else equal, than one that doesn't.

To understand how the PI approaches this ideal, notice feedback's similarity to something we're familiar with: grading. Above all, both are evaluative. In addition, the hardest assignments to grade are the ones requiring complex subjective evaluations, just like creative writing feedback. Content analysis is the scientific term for conducting these kinds of evaluations. (Google for more info.) Essentially, this technique, which is inherent to successful grading systems, depends on what we teachers generally call rubrics: clear rules for examining and scoring.

Using the PI

The PI, at heart, is a rubric for evaluating stories. Again, take a look at the image or interactive version: bardsy.com/stories/pub-index. At the top, you'll see the PI distills much of the conventional wisdom regarding what makes a story great. You're familiar with the first six elements: character, world, conflict, theme, plot and language. For precision's sake, as well as comprehensiveness and consistency, the elements are further divided into dimensions. (Spoiler alert!) Character, for one, is broken down into description, backstory and agency.

Bardsy PUBLISHABILITY INDEX™

		A GOOD STORY HAS:	A GREAT STORY ALSO HAS:
CHARACTER	DESCRIPTION	☐ Identifiable and plausible actors, human or not	☐ Authentic characters who come to imagined life
	BACKSTORY	☐ Main characters with pasts that inform their identities	☐ Relevant histories that spur individual change and action
	AGENCY	☐ Characters who manifest through thoughts and choices	☐ Clear, cumulative character development
WORLD	PHYSICALITY	☐ Descriptive details that create a complete setting	☐ A world that readers can imagine being within
	CULTURE	☐ A defined society	☐ A social environment with key features fully realized
	CONTINUITY	☐ No unintended anomalies	☐ Intentional inconsistencies that enrich the setting
CONFLICT	GOAL-STAKE	☐ Discernible motivations for all actions	☐ Friction that readily intensifies stakes
	OPPOSITION	☐ Obstacles that impede goals	☐ Situations that make discord inevitable
THEME	CLARITY	☐ Some recognizable message	☐ An organic, overarching message
	RELEVANCE	☐ A relatable message	☐ A profound impact
PLOT	INCITING	☐ A specific incident that tees up events	☐ An initial event that sets expectations and creates momentum
	RISING	☐ A logical sequence of events tied to advancing narrative	☐ Compounding events that compel engagement
	CLIMAX	☐ An obvious emotional peak	☐ A culmination of tension realized in a defining moment
	FALLING	☐ No unintended loose ends	☐ A managed moment that allows readers to recover
	RESOLUTION	☐ A clear ending whether open or closed	☐ A satisfying and impactful conclusion
LANGUAGE	EXPRESSION	☐ Apt word choice and syntax	☐ Stimulating vocabulary and phrasing
	VOICE	☐ A consistent style	☐ A distinctive, evocative style
	MECHANICS	☐ No mistakes in grammar, punctuation, etc.	☐ Purposeful and impactful construction throughout
COHESION	ENVIRONMENT	☐ Characters who fit world and vice versa	☐ A synergistic interaction between characters and world
	VERACITY	☐ A Solid connection between conflict and theme	☐ Conflict and theme locked into a mutually reinforcing spiral
	INTEGRATION	☐ No incompatibility between elements	☐ A productive orchestration of all elements
	DYNAMICS	☐ No unintended discontinuities between events	☐ Unfolding events that exert a magnetic push or pull
	RESONANCE	☐ Events that correspond with conflict and theme	☐ Sufficient impetus from events to deliver a powerful message

For more precision, each dimension contains two criteria, labeled "good" and "great." Thus, the PI starts with 18 dimensions, each with two criteria.

Besides the familiar five elements and language, you'll find another element you've been hearing a lot about: cohesion. The PI treats it as an equal of the other elements because it's so important. The PI assesses cohesion along five dimensions: environment, veracity, integration, dynamics and resonance. Within each, the criteria call for assessing how well your elements synergize.

To evaluate your story or chapter, go through the list. Strive to evaluate your word objectively to increase your chances at producing a *publishable* work. Read the criteria for each dimension, first "good," then "great," asking whether or not the criteria is present or absent. Making this kind of yes or no, binary judgment helps produce reliable evaluations. After some practice, you'll find these decisions can be made quickly because they tap directly into the story in your head.

To illustrate, the character backstory dimension calls for your beings to have a "past that contributes to their identity" to be considered good. If, after reflection, you determine this statement is applicable, check this item. If not, move down to the next dimension. Then, if you're able to check off "good," consider the "great" criterion, which is defined as "relevant histories that spur individual development and action." (You should know, right?) If you're able to check the great box, congratulate yourself, and continue your review.

For a given story, such as an 85 thousand word novel, move down the list, reflecting, checking boxes as you (or your reviewer) go. Make notes, separately or using our interactive system, as needed. Getting more checks is unquestionably better than getting less. If you find a particular criteria unclear or less than valuable, reach out. Overall, the "great" checks reliably identify your writing's strengths, freeing you to focus on the other dimensions, especially those where the story hasn't satisfied the "good" criteria.

You can see why we think the PI is comprehensive; it includes every aspect a great story needs. Again, feel free to reach out if you think something is missing, and we'll consider it for future editions.

Ultimately, the PI's value can be found in its utility. It may take time to get comfortable with the PI and to integrate it into your practice. Of course, you don't have to use it; it's voluntary. We wholeheartedly endorse adding it to your writing practice. Nearly every author will find it to be good food for thought at the very least. For the purposes of this guide, we're going to examine the three dimensions covering character: description, backstory and agency. These three tasty morsels cover every aspect of *publishable* characters; the remainder of this guide is devoted to meeting their criteria.

Chapter 06

Description: Compose your Complex, Integrated Being

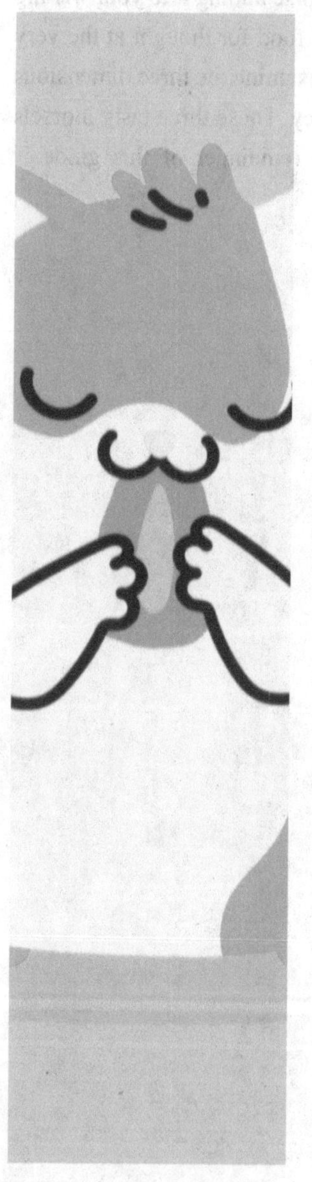

Publishability Index™ Goals:

(Good) Identifiable and plausible actors, human or not

(Great) Authentic characters who come to imagined life

PREVIEW

1. Unlike readers, you must consciously construct characters to serve a story.

2. Readers only relate to integrated (authentic), complex (investable) beings.

3. Construction can follow two steps: composition and blending.

4. Bardsy's Character Equation composes a being from three sources: author self-donation, cultural knowledge, like stereotypes, and aspects of people you know (referents).

5. Use interactions to blend your composition into a functional simulacrum before writing.

Our foundation is complete (yay!). This background opens the door to honing in on creating *publishable* characters. This framework also facilitates testing your creations. Let's review: characters are important (again, duh); they must be authentic and investable; and, your reader's ongoing investment brings them to life. Further, they exist within and for your story, so they have to perform and be evaluated in context. Successful characters ultimately reward your efforts by prompting grokking, a meld between reader and character. Grokking, in turn, leads to sales.

Here comes this foundation's pay off: this guide's last three chapters use this base to specify how to meet the standards set on PI's three character dimensions: description, agency and backstory. First, we'll cover how to create your beings. Next, we'll go over how to present them to readers. And, we'll conclude by showing how to foster their lives in a way that suits your story.

Conscious Creation

The main idea is that setting up your creations entails envisioning your being and firming up their simulacrum while keeping your ultimate goal - to produce a coherent novel - in mind. This process, indeed, is coherence's first stage: a character appears in your head. At the same time, imagining your character into being prefigures the path your readers will follow when they meet them. As you know, they respond to introductions by spinning up and, with incentive, developing a simulacra. So, your authoring starts with the same undifferentiated proto-person. Then, this being congeals and morphs into a specific someone, who you can relate to as a person. So far so good.

Unlike readers, however, authors need to be much more aware of the process leading to your being. Person perception for readers is mostly automatic. Put another way, readers take your being as given, and go from there with little to no self-monitoring. Authors, in contrast, can't sit back and watch this process unfold (contrary to some advice). You must consciously construct a being who serves your story. Creating entails shaping, juggling and revising them, more or less painstakingly, throughout your project. Inspiration and / or testing may force you to erase them and start from scratch, as well. Changing modes from passenger to driver, from automatic to manual, calls for directions. You need to know where you're headed. So, what's the aim of this endeavor? Or, using this guide's terms, how do we go about making authentic, investible beings?

Until now, we've explored authenticity from the reader's point of view. This review concludes a fictional being's authenticity comes from engaging the mental machinery humans use to relate to others. The primary advice which follows from this conclusion is to step back and allow the process to unfold. But, that isn't enough to construct your being — you have to get the ball rolling. We've deferred discussion of creating your characters until now.

This chapter on description lays out how to set up your creations. It starts this how to with a discussion of personhood, then reveals a fairly foolproof method to describe any person — an equation for fictional characters — which can govern the creation of your beings. This formula provides a recipe to use in character construction. Of course, ingredients by themselves are insufficient, so our discussion moves to mixing these ingredients together, blending them into an authentic being. We'll end with four helpful exercises you can use before, during and after you write.

Who are you? (Who, who, who, who)

You've undoubtedly heard great characters are complex, flawed and so forth. This conventional wisdom upholds these qualities as engagement's prerequisites. We've dismissed this advice, naming authenticity as a superior, more productive criteria. However, authenticity is a goal, so it only covers where you want to end up, not what you must do to get there. Let's start with the obvious: authors have a greater burden than readers, the junior partners in your novel's experience. This begs a question: what exactly is the additional responsibility? Put another way, what can you do for your character before you start writing and what must you do before you finish? Notice, this question indicates you can start writing before a character is fully developed, but they must reach this level before you can polish your manuscript. The answer is: you have to construct an integrated (underline those words: construct and integrated) being.

Have you ever met a simpleton? Probably not; this derogatory term describes one who struggles so much that they're not functional. It, for example, describes non-player videogame characters (NPCs), "beings" whose behavior is limited to following strict rules. Behind this insult is a denial of personhood. In conventional writing theory, the simpleton concept is associated with the advice to add complexity. A highly detailed character must be functional, right? Yet, the injunction against backstory teaches adding complexity won't achieve authenticity; in fact, it's not even necessary. If it's not relevant, extra detail translates to more mess. What you really need is thoughtful detail; this thinking leads to a key concept: integration. Put simply, an integrated being is holistic in the sense that they contain no thoughtless, i.e. irrelevant, detail. Similarly, to be integrated, the being you're autuering has to have enough, complementary details to be equivalent to a human. (We'll probe aliens below.)

Authenticity Implies Integration

An integrated being resembles a pocket watch, the old-fashioned kind. You've seen those, or google if you haven't. All the little gears, springs and levers come together to serve a single purpose: to tell time. In the same way, your creation's various details (like facets in the Comprehensive Character Developer — remember, it's also available online: https://bardsy.com/character) must come together to instantiate them. Like a pocket watch, if the details don't mesh or are incomplete, the personhood doesn't form. Notice, for the nth time, real people don't suffer from this problem. They're authentic — by default — because they exist. Bottom line: your authorial priority is to produce a real-person equivalent simulacrum for their fictional being, which translates to achieving personhood.

Building this mental model allows your character to do what they have to do, to fulfill their function as an element of your novel. So long as their simulacrum stays together, i.e. your writing doesn't destroy their beingness, you and eventually your reader treat them as real people. With intact personhood, you and your audience can describe them, talk to them, gossip about them and predict their behavior. In short, simulacra make any human interaction possible for your characters.

Our discussion of confusion confirms integration's import. Recall specifically the caution against having your beings make unexplained choices, literally to have them act out of character. Integration's necessity reveals another reason for this caution. An integrated being can't do anything unexplained or act out of character. (Cue the Love and Rockets song: going against nature is part of nature, too). Why? Because a person remains a person before, during and after every single act. In other words, unless said act blows them apart, your integrated being is always a being. You can effectively harmonize any random action you can dream up back into the simulacrum. In turn, harmonization sets a new baseline. We react the same way in our social lives. Should a friend unexpectedly stab you in the back, they're still a person. Their choice has made you more wary, perhaps permanently altering your feelings. They, for one, may no longer be your friend. Yet, they're still an integrated being. The unexpected action reveals new information but isn't out of character. It casts a new light on their existing character.

Going Beyond Reality Drives Investment

There's a last, vital aspect of fictional personhood that calls for a reminder: going past the real. Put simply, your characters have to be entertaining, i.e. not boring. Of course, this imperative ties to investability. Try to name a successful novel with a boring lead; they're vanishingly rare. Why take this risk? We've talked about investability, including how it arises through identification and circumstance. Let's build on this point.

The relationship between fictional beings and readers is far more intense than those reality offers. Our ability to access their thoughts, like *Don Quixote*'s, lets readers know, and ideally join, them at a level our actual counterparts can't match. Your burden is to make reading rewarding, and it's heavy. How many people's minds would you like to enter? A few certainly for curiosity's sake. Once the novelty wears off, however, you can probably count the number of people you'd be willing to grok on one hand (maybe two for humanitarians). This isn't a "hell is other people" claim, a misanthrope's concern that humans aren't worth knowing. Rather, it's a claim about tedium. Novels have to offer some type of escape, a version of life which is in some way better or more exciting.

You've heard it's hard to write super intelligent characters because most authors aren't geniuses. Few people technically are. Likewise, every science fiction aficionado knows it's hard to write aliens. Being more interesting than real has the same flavor. We all can't be Hemingway; most working authors lead pretty boring lives (no offense). And, even if you're unusually captivating, it's not enough. You have to ensure your fictional being is attention worthy. And, of course, they must also serve your story.

Two Step Birth: Composition and Blending

So, how do we create such a wondrous being? Not to be flippant, but the answer is very carefully. You construct them. Naturally, the process starts with a simulacrum which grows through elaboration — the way everyone comes to know anyone. However, the author's role is anything but natural. Real people aren't constructed. *Publishable* characters, in contrast, must be built, developed or whatever word you choose. We'll talk more about the particulars later. Suffice to say, your creative act isn't piece by piece bricklaying (as some templates promote). Instead, your duty is akin to the one attributed to Michelangelo: I saw the angel in the marble and carved until I set him free. You need to compose your character as a singular, whole piece. Yes, it sounds paradoxical, how can you compose a whole? Try this metaphor. Composing a character begins like cooking a stew; toss in some meat, vegetables and spices to suit your taste. Unlike stew, you must also blend them. The blending is critical! Your completed character should resemble pureed stew with a single uniform taste. Sounds gross, sure. The point is nothing in the final product is separable. Composition ends when your being reaches the creamy smoothness of integrated personhood.

The blending is needed to meet our twin prerequisites. First, you have to meet the authenticity challenge via the ability to hold them in mind as an integrated being. You can see this being as the angel trapped in marble. Second, you have to prompt the grokking we've talked so much about. That's investability. This challenge can be met by concentrating on relevance, chipping away at the marble, so the right angel comes out. It sounds daunting, and it is, but there's less to it than this call to action might engender. We're spending time repeating these standards and warnings to make sure you don't miss anything vital. By aiming for perfection, you'll pass the threshold for good to develop truly great beings .

As you read this, you probably have many characters in mind. That's wonderful. You've thought about them, meaning you already possess corresponding simulacra. And, if you don't, you know how easy it is to spin up dozens more. From these acorns, mighty oaks shall emerge. The first need to be fleshed out (pun intended) to the level of personhood. The next part details this process: describing your being in order to pin down who they are.

A bit of obviousness in case you're not paying attention: this PI dimension goes beyond physical description, what a detective asks: height, weight and so on. It's about wholly describing a person. In addition, as you should foresee, psychology comes first; after all, we're in the novel writing business. Thus, the description criteria concerns how well readers can know your characters as people.

After basics — a name and a curt physicality — the plan is to encourage you to put plenty of thought into your character's composition. Through these tasks, you'll select and automatically integrate detail. At some point, you'll also have to make choices, basically deciding who they are as well as who they aren't. We'll save these lessons on relevancy for the next chapter, the Backstory PI dimension. Then, in the final chapter — the Agency PI dimension — we'll do some cooking, letting your brain mostly subconsciously mix them to a whole. We'll end with a check to ensure they're ready. (You could say we'll perform a taste test.)

Step 1: Bardsy's Character Equation

The following equation dictates how to compose (as well as de and recompose) your beings. The term equation may put off mathphobes; if so, please think of it as a recipe. The sense of determinism, the idea an equals sign entails causality, may distance others. Feat not. We're going to use this equation to play with your characters. It works because it covers a hundred percent of what you need and not because it's the only way to approach fictional beings.

Here it is (big drumroll), Bardsy's Character Equation: a fictional being equals you — the author — plus universal and individuating information. Expanding, your character has three parts. First, there's a slice of you in them. Second, there's the cultural information you and your reader add, mainly stereotypes and archetypes. And, third, there's the spice, specifics you pull in to make them individuals. The third part is the newest, so we'll focus there and introduce how to use referents.

Notice, backstory isn't part of the equation. We're describing the whole being as they exist in the now. The backstory we'll add must arise organically from this person's makeup.

Character Component 1: Author Self-donation

All auteurs leave traces of themselves in their works. Novelists are no different. There's no way around it. Human bodies hold our brains prisoner, constraining us to a narrow view of the outside world. Being someone else, let alone perfectly taking their perspective is literally impossible. The best you can do is to pretend, to roleplay. Thus, the "hard to write geniuses or aliens" idea generalizes to "hard to write others." Put another way, you can't eliminate the intersection between two Venn diagram circles: the ones for you and for your character. So, why fight it? Be like the willow and bend to this truth. Accept the fact that you'll necessarily seep into your characters. Then, past acceptance, take advantage of the you in them (while safeguarding your offspring's identity).

So what advantages can be gleaned from unavoidable self-insertion? Accessibility comes first. You are you; writing you has none of the costs associated with roleplaying someone else. For most people, this modality, e.g. your thoughts, dialogue and choices, transfers more directly to the page. At another level, recordings of your experience are more accurate than inventions. A painter, for instance, probably writes about painting more intimately. A historian would do less research for historical fiction. This ease applies across autobiography. A novel about childhood trauma, like the death of a parent, would be more credible (or maybe different) from someone with that familiarity. Then, there's motivation. The urge to write may come from sharing your story or delivering your message. Your novel offers an avenue toward these goals.

This edge doesn't imply that you can't take on unfamiliar subjects; indeed, you might find those attractive. Still, authors with an applicable background have a head start. There should be no shame in using this advantage. Besides boosting marketing, odds are you'll produce a better story. Thus, the one thing you shouldn't do (in this respect) is to forbid yourself from using this resource. Such self-handicaping would be akin to learning a different language to write and, then, translating it back to English. Imagine, instead, how much easier it is to write someone who comes from an aspect of yourself. In short, the saying "write what you know" holds.

Of course, autobiography can go too far. The Mary Sue / Gary Stu trope, i.e. writing a perfected version of yourself into a story, exists in part as a caution. Who wouldn't want to play Lancelot (google this early superhero), the honorable and capable knight, slaying dragons and rescuing kingdoms. But, what makes him intriguing is his fatal attraction to Guinviere, the king's wife. In other words, Lancelot — the "perfect" person — is inauthentic and boring. Further, adding this misplaced lust flaw wouldn't satisfy contemporary audiences. Folk versions of Lancelot were not delivered via novels. Only an interesting Lancelot could carry a book, one with motivations and constraints. These struggles would make his choice to hook up with Guinviere worth our attention. His cardboard version, in contrast, can only be a minor character. In the same way, a Mary Sue won't arouse the interest leading to empathy that a *publishable* main character demands.

Too much self-insertion has additional dangers, best seen in "political" novels. Ayn Rand, for instance, delivered polemics in thinly disguised versions of herself. Regardless of your ideology, no novel which features a twenty or so page speech on capitalism's virtues could be considered good writing. Heinlein presents a more interesting case. His *Starship Troopers*, for example, is sometimes said to be extolling facism and militarism. Similarly, some believe *Time Enough for Love* endorses incest. Reviewing his background and desire to court controversy makes either view unlikely. Still, he offers a cautionary tale. Controversy for its own sake seldom proves rewarding over the long haul. If you doubt this claim, look more closely at the "controversy's" audience to see the actual value on offer.

How can you effectively incorporate yourself into your being? The initial advice follows from our mandate: build an integrated character and a coherent story, testing as you go. Of course, you deserve specifics. The Character Equation approach to self-insertion calls for decomposing yourself and then selecting a few, appetizing chunks for your being. (Henceforth, the stew metaphor is banished.) You need self-awareness, which most authors happily have. The idea behind decomposition is to ensure that the path from you to your being isn't straight. Thus, they won't be an extrapolation of you, they'll be qualitatively different.

In performing the transplant, be precise. You want to surgically select and move one part at a time. In addition, you want that part to have psychological leverage. While it's easy enough to give a character your hair or educational pedigree, the more effective donation is part of your attitude toward life. For example, give your character your sense of humor or the same affection for dogs. You can use other aspects, too, like your profession or geographical familiarity. Whatever slice you pick should be enough to inform your being's thoughts and behaviors. Of course, you can borrow multiple parts. Along with slices of your personality and experience, you could include a love of music or food. Meanwhile, by being precise and setting boundaries on the transfer, the implants will be tightly controlled, permitting you to fully exploit yourself with little risk of self-indulgence.

In sum, your character must be constructed to be "independent" of you although you're necessarily part of them. Remaining conscientious in their construction helps create a being who's different from a duplicate. You can further rely on the equation to limit yourself to roughly a third of your character. As one ingredient in the mix, your character is not you plus X (an extrapolation), but you finely blended with all else. We will continue this discussion of independence; for the moment, rest assured there will be ways to assess how well your transplants take.

Character Component 2: Universal Cultural Knowledge, aka Stereotypes and Archetypes

The second part of the Character Equation acknowledges the part readers play. It does so by anticipating your reader's contribution. (Experiencing a novel is a co-creative act.) So, in creating your being, plan for what readers will bring. Naturally, their simulacrum can't be haphazardly filled with available junk. Instead, their contribution should be organized into bundles with nice, clear labels, where each label names a specific stereotype or archetype.

Envision this as an ice cream shop label, which allows the reader to envision how their dessert will taste. For example, they know Rocky Road has marshmallows and nuts, so seeing this label prompts them to anticipate those ingredients. In this way, potential information floods in whenever readers detect your being carries a particular stereotype (or archetype). These details, as we know, can be extremely useful in terms of fleshing out your character; nevertheless they can also be counterproductive. The key is to manage reader contributions, basically to get the label right. The same character composition advice regarding self-insertion applies: be conscientious, limit the cultural import to roughly a third of your character and blend well. Testing, though, is more important; you know yourself better than you know the cultural associations readers might bring. Thus, it's necessary to pinpoint readers' donations and to confirm they align with your vision.

We've covered how stereotyping works. Relatively few words cause readers to identify your creature as a type. Recognition of said type, in turn, causes them to tap into cultural stores. Then comes the potential to import these details en masse to nascent simulacra. In technical terms, the category activates, triggering a possibly substantial elaboration that follows from your being's group membership.

Controlling this process intelligently is absolutely critical. The main danger, as you know, is inadvertent triggers, where your seeds prompt unintended elaborations. Let's take a fantasy example. Say your character "codes" as an ogre with a pig nose and greenish skin. The reader would elaborate their simulacrum with ogre-ish traits, such as brutish behavior and an eagerness to fight. These additions work well when they fit your being's composition. They might also set up a productive plot point; if your story has them defy their stereotypical expectations, for instance. Shrek, the relatively kind ogre, serves as a good example. What doesn't work is not realizing you've created an ogre, triggering expectations and ignoring their implications. Thus, it takes lots of context to make a beautiful princess fall in love with an ugly brute. If the story is lacking, the reader disconnects.

Heed the "be intentional" advice. Then, use stereotypes to lay a character's groundwork. The right words can unleash copious detail. Moreover, this information comes from the reader, so it qualifies as investment. Naturally, this requires knowing your audience's culture. See your words as keys, and be cautious yet optimistic about what doors they unlock. And, when you unlock them, know what you'll find. If you have any doubt whatsoever, test. (You should always have doubts.) You can think about archetypes the same way.

Character Component 3: Individuation, Distinctiveness and Specificity from Referents

To this point, the output of the equation is parts of you plus what you induce readers to bring. The risk is that this being is too generic, so you need more. Specifically, your being needs specificity — not complexity. Hence, this recipe's last component addresses how to create more distinct individuals.

In pursuing individuality, keep in mind uniqueness is overrated. Snowflakes, of course, would disagree. Let's think about these bits of ice for a moment. The complex, random ways their birth conditions, such as temperature, humidity, turbulence, molecular alignment and more, combine gives rise to endless variation, an infinite number of possible snowflakes. Indeed, they're unique in that no two are alike. Poke beneath this majesty, however, and you'll see Ecclesiastes, "there is no new thing under the sun," has the last word. For all their variety, a snowflake is a snowflake is a snowflake. You may enjoy examining them, but sooner or later their putative diversity grows repetitious. Each starts with a waterdrop and undergoes the same crystallization process, which tightly constrains the final product. This dependence on channeled randomness robs meaning from their differences. In this way, snowflakes are unique but generic.

In creating *publishable* characters, the proper goal is for them to be meaningfully distinct. Convenience is this aim's first benefit; you want readers to identify and remember your creations. More characters, all else equal, lead to a more taxing novel. This goes double if your beings are similar. Have you watched a TV show whose characters looked alike, generic men of the same age, hair style and build? Think Band of Brothers or Peaky Blinders. Brilliant series, but it takes a few episodes before you can reliably name each face. Writing magnifies this issue. When reading, a lack of individuation can devolve to annoyance and confusion. The distinctiveness' convenience extends to you. An individual is easier for you to know and track.

How can you make simulacra distinct? The first two parts of the formula don't offer much of an answer. The you part are but slices, consciously limited and nowhere near a complete person. Likewise, the cultural part is universal and, therefore, heading toward the generic. Meanwhile, as mentioned, there's nothing new under the sun, meaning that setting your sights on creating a perfectly distinct being, someone with no similarities to anyone else, is a fool's errand. Such attempts are also likely to land in the uncanny valley (and fail at authenticity). This holds true for special gifts, as well. Too often authors endow their proto beings with superpowers. Like Rain Man or the "chosen" one, these characters benefit from deus ex machina; the author's wand elevates them to uniqueness. Yet, they are simultaneously inhuman. The referent idea, in contrast, encourages you to root through the catalog of regular human features and select a few to mix into your constructions. This spice, if you will, sets your being apart as an individual.

Thus, the Character Equation's third component concerns specifics, qualities you add to foster individuation. A "referent" is someone, perhaps fictional, you know well, well enough for you to be able to decompose them and steal their parts for your character. (Sounds macabre, but it works.) This term captures how to find and harness these factors. Here, we're doubling down on the "write what you know" wisdom. Familiarity and intentionality facilitates this transfer, which helps you to write authentic beings. As you'd expect, the extraction process parallels the one used on yourself, so the same advice applies: be precise and set limits on what you take.

To use a referent: choose a being you know who has an intriguing feature, then observe — and trace — how it permeates their being, how it affects their thoughts and behavior, for example. This eliminates the need to imagine mental repercussions or figure out how these attitudes connect because the answer is under your nose, a human cheat sheet. Albert Einstein illustrates. Culturally, he's a one person almost stereotype / archetype for genius. His name, in this capacity, evokes expectations. He embodies opaque brilliance (the math chalkboards), absent-mindedness (forgets to comb his hair) and irreverence (the famous tongue picture). However, the referent concept explicitly avoids these simple associations. Put another way, referents are not stereotypes and don't involve cultural knowledge!

The referent relationship has to be sharp and intimate. Why? Think about what you could steal from Einstein. Maybe hair? But, you know little beyond that it looked unkept at one phase of his life. You can't appreciate the messy hair psychologically. Early pictures reveal better grooming. Was his later look a conscious decision, something which escaped notice or a grooming product failure? Research may yield a suspicion, not definitive insight. Contrast this with an intimate acquaintance. They have good and bad hair days, and you've witnessed both. Observation, including conversation, brings awareness of their attitude toward each. One friend may fixate on getting their hair perfect, while others couldn't care less. This aspect further pervades their being to varying degrees. Someone born with "great hair" doesn't have certain worries. Further, their hirsute halo may boost self-confidence. They may also be haughty or dismissive of others' grooming regimens.

Crucially, you shouldn't pose, dig through and answer these psychological questions. Referents allow you to steal rather than imagine. Try to capture a full slice of the target being, with its inbuilt individuation, and add it to your character. To illustrate, let's preview how we'll build Pat the firefighter. We want to add a terrible temper to this being, so the thought is to use a child as a referent. Further, this can't be any generic child, it has to be one we've personally witnessed. (From this point on the example will be vague to preserve anonymity.) When their temper triggers, their face scrunches in a unique way signaling things are about to blow. You may rush in, but it's too late as a chain reaction has started. It slowly gathers, eyes twitching and body jerking, until an outburst erupts. Minutes later it subsides in little aftershocks. Finally, note how this disposition pervades their individuality. In other words, the temper isn't only about the incident but how it affects their life. For example, people they know walk on eggshells, or they feel shame afterward. All this becomes part of Pat.

This technique generates authenticity by infusing specific humanity. After all, you're using an actual, realized being as a donor. The more direct experience you have with your target, the better. Of course, a good heist requires forethought and keen observation. Like grafting a fruit tree branch, the "scion" material has to be precisely cut and blended into your creation. Start small at first. With practice, you can be more imaginative and produce wonderful hybrids drawn from multiple people. What you can borrow, and from whom, depends on your opportunities — and what your story demands. The better you know someone the smoother the theft. Immediate family and friends are good targets. At the same time, the psychological transparency of certain historical or fictional characters is attractive, too. Look for components with maximal psychological leverage.

In this vein, don't "tack on" quirks, the grab should be wide and deep. Consider compulsive hand washing. Over the course of a novel, continually citing their search for a nearby sink would be cringeworthy. Rather, a fruitful theft would get to the root of the behavior, presumably germaphobia, and vary the way it's expressed. Germaphobia could also inform every choice and manifest throughout their behavior. Better still that trait should subtly (not heavy-handedly) help propel the story.

Step 2: Shake it Up!

The next step is to integrate your being, which is fundamental to relatability. The premise is integrated beings are individuals while everything else — no matter how well composed — is an object. Like snowflakes, humans are combinations of disparate parts. Unlike snowflakes, each human's genesis is neither random nor as tightly constrained. So many inputs come together, in an overwhelming variety of ways, into a human being that they are more than unique; each exists as a distinct individual. To say no two are alike is an understatement. Moreover, you — and every other being — is a gestalt entity. (Try saying it fast.)

In recognizing a person, we're "hard-wired" to see them in their entirety. The reverse also holds; when we see this type of entity, we recognize them as a person. Personhood and wholeness are tied together, even though that fact seldom occurs to us in the wild. Author's beings, in contrast, are artificial. This presents a challenge: turning your selection of disparate ingredients into a whole. From the opposite angle, the aim is to avoid producing a Frankensteinish monstrosity (though he is a fantastic character.) In this metaphor, the monster's seams, bolts and poorly matched parts represent failure. Such a being is neither authentic nor investable. To escape this fate, thoroughly blend your ingredients. In short, a natural individual is a seamless blend of nearly infinite influences, and an artificial being must attain seamlessness to be knowable, relatable and interactable — capacities all ordinary people have.

Initially, we're looking to see whether the collected pieces could come together. This is not to say people don't contain contradictions. Recall each of us contains Whitman's multitudes. The issue is whether a person with these pieces is feasible. Harken back to the cautionary Mary Sue. Imagine shopping for every attractive aspect humanity offers. This cart starts with physical beauty, extreme intelligence, athletic grace and innumerable talents. Then, we'd add every virtue, such as compassion, humility and discipline, You get the idea. When done, we put these parts into a human-shaped box, a simulacrum. Enough shoving and what do we get? Perhaps a kind of god. Not a Greek god; they're imperfect, nor the old testament's angry geezer. Maybe it's Buddah. In any case, this god-like thing isn't human; it's not a person.

Not So Fast on the CCD

Time for a short warning: like every guide to creating characters this one includes a template. Our Comprehensive Character Developer is featured at this guide's end, and it's fantastic. Once again, the online version, with printable sheets and archive, is at: https://bardsy.com/character. It covers nearly every imaginable way to describe a being. (It's roughly three times deeper than the next best one available, too.) Yet, this wealth of possibilities offers danger. You should only use templates like this to inspire or to flesh out, not to make a list. Constructing a character is not like making a sandwich, you can't keep piling on things you like and hope they will taste good. So, don't go overboard; begin with a few items (see our Pat example), then use the Character Equation to gradually expand. Most importantly, finish reading this guide before you face temptation. Let's repeat the goal: to produce a simulacrum that could come from an actual person in service of your story.

At this point, a speculative fiction author could object. Let's hear them out. Maybe they say "whatever, my character isn't human." In other words, I can throw in the kitchen sink, so long as I declare my being surpasses human bounds. They can't. More precisely, they can't and expect readers to relate to their assemblage. Science fiction, fantasy or otherwise, your being absolutely must engage the universal person perceiving machinery. True, there are alien entities in masterworks. Look at them closely. You'll see many aren't people; they're objects. In other words, they don't count. Some apparently alien entities are really brothers from another mother, humans in disguise. Put another way, they're sufficiently peoply that readers relate to them. Works from Star Trek to Hail Mary, for instance, star a parade of sapient rocks who evoke sympathy, even grokking, because they provoke simulacra which meet our standard. (Commander Data also falls into this category.)

Know that there are limits on what readers will accept. Think back to the uncanny valley. Violations of human norms leads to loathing and disgust. Your Mary Sue might not cause such a strong reaction; nevertheless, it behooves you to create a person, which means checking your parts' joint suitability. Another way to look at this mandate is to make sure your being is not too much of anything. If you find yourself drawing outside these lines, rein yourself in and / or get a second opinion.

Mixing Mechanics

Blending is the next step toward integration. With a viable set of components, mixing them takes less work than it may appear. It's an almost automatic process, a side benefit that comes from interacting with your proto-creature. And, you must really interact. The more you treat them as a person, the sooner they will emerge as one. It's your goal, to form an integrated model of this being in your head. So draw them, talk to them, have them tell a joke and so forth. You aren't looking into any one trait or aspect; you're engaging with their entirety like a real person. This process is almost a performance, a rehearsal for life, in which you play two roles: you and them. It's productive, for example, to question them, even if it seems foolish. Authors who use puppets or pictures achieve remarkable results. As your interactions accumulate, your creation coalesces, taking on the mantle of personhood and coming to life.

Where exactly is the blending? Again, it's a byproduct of these exercises. Your coalesced creation is blended. Further, the blend includes all the components you intended. Or, — and this is vital — maybe not. If your being comes together without a part you wanted, chances are it doesn't fit or is unnecessary. You've subconsciously ejected it from the developing simulacrum. If you really want an aspect included, i.e. your story depends on it, you may have to start over. Why? In the first place, readers are likely to reject that piece, too. So, you need to rethink from scratch, reevaluating everything the original recipe lists. A lack of fit comes from elements somehow clashing. You can also reiterate the problem irrelevant detail presents. Remember, gluing on a limp, a drawl or some flaw in an attempt to make your character more real doesn't work. Such attempts are more than likely to backfire. The extraneous component stands out, separate from your mix. Thus, you risk producing a caricature, an exaggerated representation, as opposed to a relatable being. This discussion of beingness continues under the heading of agency.

Example: Composing and Blending a Character

Let's work up a character to practice using the Character Equation. We'll bring back Pat the firefighter to model.

Whether character or other story elements come first, at some point — and ever after — story coherence takes over as your main concern. To make this example simple, let's sketch the story. Pat's tale concerns firefighting and bravery. You can see how this accommodates the stereotype. Our protagonist's name and career have already spun up your simulacrum. To add specificity, the story focuses on another kind of bravery; Pat's facing retirement. Of course, standard bravery — running into burning buildings — remains in the background (fingers crossed for a movie deal). Hence, the outline makes age a contextually critical characteristic. So, Pat's 62. To finish setup, add a look with gender. He's male and in pretty good shape, albeit stocky. Not a candidate for greatest story ever told, but this outline sets the stage for the equation's use. Moreover, our mind's eye can loosely picture Pat, as you'll see, that really helps.

So, what can we take from the author? We'll use this guide's putative sense of humor, i.e. snarky movie and music references, and a love of dogs. Our story-driven intentions are realized in both aspects. We've, first, narrowed the genre to comedy. Pat's also getting a dog sidekick to support his role. We'll decide whether the pup will be a major or minor character later; for now, he gets a name: Mac. In case you're wondering, humans typically have simulacra for pets; they see them as people. Neither of these aspects should be hard to transplant. The humor comes naturally, though the jokes may not land, and the dog experience sits ready. There's always a risk of too much autobiography, so that would be monitored were this a real project.

Potential imports from stereotypes and archetypes begin with what firefighting could contribute. The theme also should heighten age's salience; being a boomer comes with loads of baggage. In addition, the realization of his boomerhood will overlap with several boomer referents, and it's purposeful. The Character Equation's three categories don't have hard borders. This spillover promotes blending, as well. Lastly, make him a grizzled warrior. Pat has been at war with fire for years; he's seen action and it shows (though exactly how remains to be seen). This archetype doesn't limit us, either; for example, maybe there's an enthusiasm about new tech. He dreams of setting up a high tech fire suppression system to score a decisive victory over his old foe. These choices, together, lead to more story, like minor character foils. Depending on who and what else enters the story, Pat's boomer warrior nature will manifest in different ways. Is he going to mentor a rookie? Perhaps he's injured and needs discipline to recover? As we'll discuss under the agency heading, successful novels bring characters to life through plot.

Finding referents isn't too hard, either. Notice they don't have to be boomers. Say Pat throws a temper tantrum. Who better to copy than a screaming child you've seen, as discussed above? Again, the referent choices depend on the story and vice versa. Pat could work in NYC a la Rescue Me, or he could reside in the Appalachian wilderness. No matter what, he will be more authentic when your models match the relevant dimension. You could scour fiction for appropriate targets, too; however, the further you move from direct experience, the more wary you need to be. You probably have to work harder to secure adequate information from watching Kurt Russell (star of Backdraft) than from conversing with a neighbor, for instance.

Blending should begin ASAP. It will work because you have a simulacrum running. Remember, we blend through interaction. Talk to Pat, put him in situations and see how he responds. Open-ended questions are especially useful. Ask him about his day, his friends and his best war story. You're not creating backstory; you're integrating Pat through knowing him. It helps for these interactions to be creative, stressful and varied. Have him walk Mac. And not a vague, here's a leash let's go. Imagine a specific situation with a real dog. Where do they walk and how? Who do they meet? Does Mac like fire hydrants? Imagination is an author's omnitool; here's the opportunity to use yours. In and outside of your writing, you'll come to know your character. Time and effort starts a feedback loop that keeps enriching your mind's simulacrum as well as your page's words. Eventually, you'll bring in volunteers who will put their shoulders to your wheel. And, try the puppet option. By the time you're ready to polish your manuscript, you'll know your character better than your best friend and maybe better than yourself.

Four More Blending Tricks

These activities can be used: to explore and learn about your character; to confirm by cementing your model of them as well as to evaluate, which means assessing whether you've put them together and blended successfully. Each seeks to encourage interaction and stabilize your simulacrum.

One: Find a Picture

Once you have loosely visualized your creature, firm up that mental image with an actual picture. You're ahead in this game if you can paint or draw. No matter your skillset, sketch your character as best you can, knowing you can update their look if the need arises. This portrait helps fix them in your mind and provides an icon on which to center your interactions. A rudimentary image works better than none at all. Those lacking this kind of talent can adapt a picture from any source. You can also use various artificial techniques.

AI's use, as of this writing, is controversial, and it should be. To digress (and leap to a conclusion), serious authors need not worry about being replaced. State of the art AI can crap out endless words, but in no way will they amount to a satisfying story, especially at longer lengths. So-called generative AI is not an auteur, an individual with vision. If anything, AI should make readers more careful about what they buy, increasing the demand for quality work. Five or ten years may make this claim ridiculous, but probably not. *Publishable* characters require real empathy from author and reader. Should artificial brains reach that point, culture as we know it won't exist.

That said, you can use AI guiltlessly for extremely limited purposes. A chat program beats a thesaurus, especially as they have fewer ads. Professional proofreading may not have long to live, either. And, as said, you can use it to draw your character. On the other hand, don't use it for covers or illustrations. This task demands auteurship, a sense of your story, something AI can't offer.

Two: Make a Recipe

Chart your character's components. A table with three rows and one column — for each major character — works well. The rows take their cue from the equation: author, stereotypes / archetypes, and referrants. Each entry should be as precise as possible. You should periodically review your recipe to see if any part has become irrelevant or if a new component has emerged. Like coherence and the MCS, keeping your characterization up to date is a necessity.

As you work through your story and come to know your beings, they'll change. Further, this is not a natural progression, as it is with humans in the real world. Alterations may come randomly and sometimes drastically. Your being's constructed nature causes this seeming haphazardness. As one of the balls you're juggling, they undergo significant adjustments with or without your attention. You shouldn't be overly concerned with their stability while your story is developing. Only after your story has crystallized, do you need a comparably fixed creation. Polishing your manuscript, on the other hand, definitely requires a firm simulacrum.

Three: Play Icebreakers

Our society has many ways for people to start knowing strangers, for example: introductions, biographies and first dates. Party games sit in this realm. You can (and should) play any you wish with your character. Try these two to start. In Two Truths and a Lie, your character dreams up two true statements and one false statement; try to see what they choose. In Would You Rather, your character has to answer fun or thought-provoking questions, like "would you rather be smarter or stronger?" The point of these icebreakers is to get your character talking; being in your story's context is a good idea.

You can use volunteers for these games, as well. Have them ask questions while you respond or vice versa. They're helpful to the extent you learn your being's outlook. Any dialogue (stay tuned for more on this topic) with your character will help fill areas their simulacrum is missing. These activities do require active awareness. You should, for instance, check to see whether your being's statements match up with your intuition. They can, at this point, say things that are out of character, which requires correction or rethinking.

Four: Borrow Professional Techniques

Ostensibly or not, authoring eventually involves roleplay. You imagine beings in a situation and let them go. It's worth trying any technique other professions use for getting into character. As repeated, avoid manufacturing backstory; instead, attempt to capture who they are in the moment. The ultimate, albeit unreachable, goal is to be them. The closer you can come to this nirvana — being them as you write — the better your words will express their thoughts and feelings and lead to empathy.

Aim not to act like them but to impersonate them. You've seen effective impersonators; through a combination of language, mannerisms or voice, audiences recognize them as somebody else. What is the difference between acting and impersonating? There's no hard line; however, think of acting as creating a fictional being. Impersonation, on the other hand, implies the target exists and is known to the audience. Thus, mimicry elicits recognition — an appreciative I know this guy. A successful impersonator offers sufficient detail for viewers to make an identification. Take these two aspects: first, the volume of information and, second, its precision, to heart. They're what you need to get from this exercise.

It goes without saying that executing this advice takes subtlety. You can't give your character a hat and be done. Take Pat; does he usually wear a bowler, a firefighting helmet or a beanie? Probably none of the above, unless he's actively fighting a fire or it's cold. Our sense of Pat mandates a ball cap, probably with a logo. The logo could be associated with his sports team or a firefighting union. Notice, the hat is part of Pat, a reflection of him. It's not an affectation and not tacked on (unless affectation is organic to the character), because it's not intrinsic to who they are. Put another way, it fits our expectations. It's something we could organically see being put on to walk Mac. Moreover, the cap is incidental. We need to mention it once or twice over the course of the novel for readers to add it to their image. Any more would be obvious and too much.

Amazingly, the ball cap could be very useful to you as an author. Think of it as a talisman that gives you the power to become Pat. Many impersonators use such devices to get into character. A professional mimic might have dozens of characters to perform. They bring each to the fore with a specific detail. Sometimes a prop or a gesture, like a posture or a catchphrase, can lock a persona in place. You can use the same trick as you write. Cartoonists, for example, often use puppets. So why not find a voice, a clothing item or a particular look which codes your character? When writing Pat, a certain head tilt with a slight squint might be exactly what it takes to engage his simulacrum and empower you to write him.

Testing for Beingness

We can't close this chapter without describing one way to test your character. This evaluation calls for more creativity from your volunteer than the retelling exercise. It also borrows from the professional techniques outlined above, so finding someone with a flare for drama or real acting experience helps. The idea is to present the components from your equation to someone and see whether they can behave as a real person in line with the identity. (You can add the output from the Comprehensive Character Developer when you reach that stage, especially if you deploy the online version's printable sheet: https://bardsy.com/character.)

A simple list or a more organized table will suffice. Here are the Character Equation prompts whose answers you'll provide to your actor. First, this person is like me because. Second, they're members of the following groups. And third, they're like these other people you know because. The last, naturally, may be difficult should your volunteer not know them. Then, give them time to think. The feedback comes from asking them questions and judging answers. Start with easy ones, like what did you have for breakfast and move on to the hard stuff. What's your life about? It's useful to present them with brief scenarios from the novel to see how they'll behave. You want to see them dialoguing easily and organically. If they don't, see if you can nudge them in the right direction. These nudges then should feed back into your being's identity. You may have to return to the equation or blending should the test not go well. Remember to have fun and thank them profusely.

In all, *publishable* characters are hybrids, finely blended combinations of the same parts every being has. A fictional being's components fall into three categories: the author, the universal, the distinct. Hence, the Character Equation asks you to precisely identify what you're taking from each source. The next goal is to solidify your being, meaning to create a simulacrum as good as the ones you use for real people. In all, then, description has two stages. First, carefully choose your ingredients and, then, blend them via imaginative interaction. Further, your character will change as your project evolves and from testing. Description, seen in this light, produces a provisional being who will develop into the one your story needs.

Chapter 07

Backstory: Let Readers Bring Your Character to Life

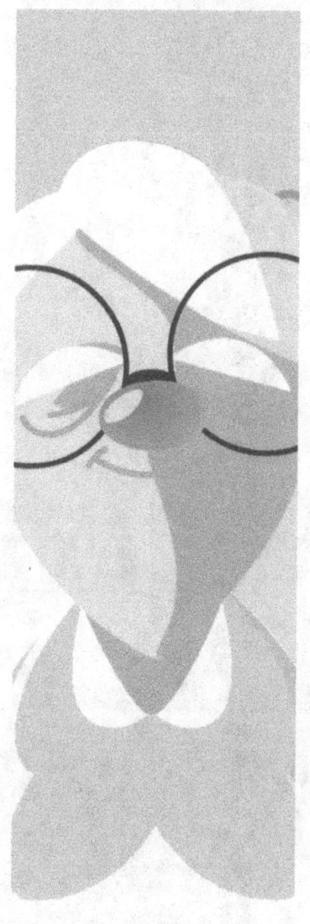

Publishability Index™ Goals:

(Good) Main characters have past that contributes to their identity

(Great) Relevant histories spur individual development and action

PREVIEW

1. After choosing words, you control the reading experience with their sequence and volume.

2. Primacy means readers remember what comes first in introductions, which shapes what comes later.

3. Backstory should be brief, relevant, and — most importantly — derived from an established identity.

4. Use your natural ability to gossip to gauge the relevance of details as you write.

5. Rank an identity's details in order of their story importance to choose introductory seeds.

By now this guide's stance on backstory should be painfully clear, explicitly: don't create an extensive history and be very careful about how much — and what — detail you add. However, this does not suggest your characters don't need some (brief and relevant) backstory; they do. Everybody, real or imagined, has a history. The main concern stems from the observation that fictional beings' histories are not organic, like yours. Knowing someone you know grew up in New York, for instance, partially governs who they are. Knowing you dreamed up a character while having breakfast doesn't accomplish the same thing. Likewise, you shouldn't break the fourth wall to say how a sibling inspired the being they're reading about. In short, the "real" history doesn't matter. Instead, you have to construct a history to fulfill your audience's curiosity about your being's origins. Further, this history has to maintain coherence.

Spoiler alert: The only way to maintain coherence is for backstory to come from identity, rather than the other way around. This reversal marks the biggest difference between fictional beings and real ones (and the biggest departure of this guide from others). Keeping this in mind, let's take stock. The previous chapter set up your character; now we move on to discuss how to transfer them from your mind to a reader's. Specifically, we're going to look at introductions. A good intro selects and presents only the most important facts from your character's identity. These facts include relevant backstory. Ideally, one long paragraph (or two short ones) elicits an accurate simulacrum, which grounds further development and brings your character to life.

Identity Comes First (Last and Always)

You always have "somebody" already in mind when dealing with fictional beings. Recall our brains are astoundingly inventive; we perceive any of our creations as beings long before we know much about them. Creating extensive backstory muddles the beingness of your being by putting the cart before the horse. Look at how fiction departs from reality. A real person's story is set in stone; we learn about them, chiefly whatever facts they share. Authors (not readers) must do the opposite for their characters. The fictional being's identity comes first. You may have created one by following the Character Equation, for example. Such beings spring from your head with no history beyond some obvious basics. Pat, for example, must have gone to a firefighting school but you know little more. Nevertheless, you can interact with him. In other words, he has an identity without history.

Still, creatures need some history if only to satisfy your readers' curiosity. Because identity comes first, you should build a matching history after you have a firm grip on who they are. This guide places description before backstory for this reason. In constructing a limited backstory, it's best not to impose facts on them; instead, let their identity guide you. This approach helps maintain your being's wholeness and your story's coherence. So, now that you have a being in hand, it's time to make history (with the ever-present caveat: everything stays in motion until the final manuscript).

Fictional Beings Establish Themselves

At first glance, it seems backstory could be addressed in the same way as stereotypes. There, the advice was to prevent counterproductive elaborations by exploring what your triggers might bring. Here, this procedure is helpful but not enough. In deducing what history led to an identity, your character's uniqueness works against you. In other words, there's no answer key to tell you what backstory is correct. Actual people don't have this problem. The social world uses what has happened to them — their history — to decide what background fits a situation. With stereotypes, asking a few people what a trigger entails produces a usable response. Your unique being, in contrast, hasn't left any footprints in the wider world.

A party game called "Exquisite Corpse" clarifies the challenge posed by not having an external reference. The fun comes from having a group collaboratively create somebody. It starts with a body template, a sheet with areas for parts: head, chest and so on. The first person draws the head, hides it by folding the paper, leaving the neck visible to connect to the chest. As you'd guess, the next person draws the chest, folds and leaves a connection. The game ends when the areas are full. The host sheet unfolds and reveals the Frankensteinian creature. Hilarity ensues!

Would you risk playing Exquisite Corpse with your character, to give readers a start and let readers chaotically add the rest? You may not believe it happens, yet it does. Beginning novelists sometimes fill first chapters with description and stop, never writing about their creation again. With nothing additional to go on, the readers default to developing the being on their own and slapdashedly pile on what comes to mind. You'll dodge this bullet easily partially thanks to this guide.

A more subtle version of this responsibility abdication warrants your attention. Put simply, it's the requirement for you to have a solid identity to work from. Once again, the challenge of maintaining an integrated person while inventing backstory mirrors the others you face. With respect to coherence, you have to keep your story elements mutually aligned even as they change. However, turning to backstory modifies this advice. To avoid messing up your character: hold your character's identity steady and write a history to fit. In short, identity comes first and last; backstory is in the middle. (We'll discuss the semantics of change in this guide's last chapter.)

What should you do when inspiration strikes? Perhaps, for instance, you dream up an exciting life event. Two options follow. First, you could add the incident to the story and adjust other elements accordingly. If so, it becomes part of the plot. (We'll hold off on discussing plotting.) Otherwise, you could decide to keep it offscreen, out of the story. This choice makes the event backstory and, critically, demands you reexamine your creation's identity. This examination can have two outcomes. On the one hand, you may find the new event to be plausible; great! Such an alignment shows you know your being. On the other hand, the event could be implausible, meaning you must reshape their identity to make it plausible for your being.

No Second Chance to Make First Impressions

After establishing an identity, sequencing is the most pressing issue in planning an introduction. Here sequence does not refer to ordering their lives birth to death but to prioritizing what readers need to know. Recognize, initially, that you can spend eons creating and blending your creature. Moreover, you're not locked into any version but the last, the creature you send to the publisher. The reader, conversely, gets one shot, a single introduction to the ultimate version.

An infamous American shampoo commercial offers this motto: you never get a second chance to make a first impression. Its pitch centers on how a dandruff speck leads to irrevocable disgust (Google). Though the ad's claim seems incredible, the slogan rings true. The first impression idea traces to Dale Carnegie, author of 1936's *How to Win Friends and Influence People.* It also features prominently in person perception research. To whet your appetite: research finds that it takes roughly a tenth of a second to evaluate a new person's trustworthiness, attractiveness, and likability. Moreover, these judgments tend to stick. It takes many subsequent encounters to change your mind after a positive (or negative) first impression. Creating a *publishable* character takes more than a good smile and a hearty handshake; we're not selling cars. Yet the principle, what comes first matters infinitely more, stands as a worthy exaggeration. This guide refers to picking seeds over and over for this reason: first impressions count. Your character's publishability depends on a successful introduction.

All the effort you put into creating an identity stands ready to support your being's intro. You need to see that instant where the reader meets them as a rubber meets the road moment. And, this moment is fragile, constrained and — above all — sudden. These aspects intertwine, so any attempt to unravel them would be counterproductive. How sudden, you ask? Let's review the research.

Numerous studies reveal how long it takes to form first impressions. Within milliseconds of seeing a face for the first time, we confidently rate the owner's attractiveness. It's not unexpected; beauty is easy to behold and all that. Besides looks, however, we make other judgements, crucially whether the face's owner is trustworthy and likable. (As you might expect, these judgments correlate.) Remarkably, then, it takes less than a tenth of a second to be predisposed toward trusting and liking a new person — or not. It's almost a reflex. In less artificial settings, mainly in-person introductions, forming these attitudes takes a bit longer — about seven seconds. Still, humans don't dawdle; much of a relationship's fate is set in the time a few breaths take. For example, less than ten seconds after introduction we tend to express confidence in our ratings as well as a readiness to act on them. Participants in these studies meet actual people, typically face to face. Other studies present written character sketches; this research shows forming impressions takes less than a page.

An Impression's Consequences

It's safe to say our opinions of others have a lot of inertia. Put another way, it takes a lot to get us to change our minds once they're made up. Authors should pay attention to first impressions' persistence, which means they affect every interaction that follows. From a different angle, our relationships — including reader to character — are like snowflakes because their starting conditions matter. A great intro likely leads to a good relationship; conversely, a bad intro probably means no relationship at all. We've all been there. You fall in love or choose a friend, then ignore the red flags past the point of rationality. Confirmation bias plays a big role in this tendency; we tend to discount or misattribute evil choices from people we like and vice versa. We'll dig into attribution, i.e. resolving who's responsible for what, in this guide's last chapter.

These first impressions run deeper than good or bad, too. We well know a simulacrum's capacity for detail. An introduction supplies only a few specifics, and we fill this person's corresponding model by building around those. Here's an added point. If we're paying attention, we may extrapolate with an eye toward seeing an integrated person. We can try, for example, to reconcile details that don't add up. Why is this northerner speaking with a southern accent? The route to reconciliation is complex and the outcome is uncertain. This means your being's first impression requires extra care.

Moving beyond the good / bad dichotomy increases the opportunity for misperception. You know the error avalanche's (see Chapter Four) dangers. We make mistakes, sometimes due to hasty extrapolation. You don't see a wedding ring and assume someone was single, for instance. Reality makes these mistakes embarrassing but correctable. It's substantially harder to correct a reader's mischaracterization. The "Curse of Knowledge" addresses this phenomenon. To understand this issue, think about a court case where a judge tells the jury to disregard a fact, for example that a defendant has prior convictions. The jury can't do it as hard as they might try, knowing the fact prevents imagining it's not true. For writers, a worst-case scenario involves messing up a clue in a mystery. Readers can't "unknow" the mistaken clue and subsequent interpretations are unfixably wrong. This lesson goes double for building a simulacrum around a mistaken impression. Authors don't have the opportunity to correct these mistakes.

Leading with (or prioritizing) the wrong information also leads to misperception. Naive authors often fail, particularly when introducing their characters, to draw sufficient attention to key facts. Continuing the mystery example: if the solution turns on a suspect's expertise with poison, the reader has to be aware of this fact before it contributes to the story's impact. Likewise, Pat's age should be obvious from page one. Why? For too many reasons, not least of which is that his age dovetails with the story's conflict, theme, world and plot. A bad Pat intro would fail to set this number in the reader's mind. Overall, any crucial specific can get lost in an infodump. It's easy to evaluate your transmission through the retelling test. And, you always should. At the same time, this advice — to lead with important details — segues to how to select the right seeds.

Making Good Impressions

Before we move to seeding, let's extend our appreciation of reading one more time. Typically, meeting someone face-to-face is a holistic experience, where we can receive input from all five senses. Reading's bandwidth, in contrast, is severely limited; generally, we go through novels (and maybe audiobooks) one word at a time. Further these words come in sequence, one after the other, as opposed to the simultaneous gestalt we normally sense. Yet, the outcome of these divergent processes is the same, a simulacrum. Thus, we have a deluge of information on one side, which immediately forms a whole, versus reading, where we're hand-fed details in an excruciatingly serial process.

This observation helps pinpoint your responsibility. Specifically, moving into the realm of words — to low bandwidth transmission — transfers filtering duty. This may sound like an odd claim for authors. Pause to think about it; it's both true and vital. Why? Because our reader's perceptual capabilities shift as they move from life to reading. Typical introductions give our brains the chance to sort through a menu of available details — extremely quickly — and snatch a few to store. Try to list all the qualities one face brings: teeth, nose, eyes, hair, expression and so forth. There are dozens, if not hundreds, of details on offer. A few get past our filter to influence evaluations and enter the corresponding memory model. In reading, the information flows so slowly that we don't need or use filters. This lack of filtering, which is traceable to readers' willingness to pay attention, allows authors to control exactly what they learn about your characters.

Filtering heavily overlaps with the concept of salience. To be salient means to be particularly noteworthy in a given context. In plain English, things are salient when they stand out and capture our attention. In a normal introduction, our brains select and keep salient details. Reflect for a moment on people you've met. You can probably associate a prominent feature with each. There's the guy with the red hair, the one with the crooked smile or the kid with the giant mole (for Austin Power's fans). Salient aspects can be less physical, too. The waiter who did magic tricks or your friend who's always sneezing. Notice how context determines what's salient. The red-haired guy who stands out in Japan becomes one more dude at a ginger convention.

When reading, the brain turns off its filter, meaning you (mostly) control salience and, therefore, what's remembered. In other words, your writing dictates what about your characters stands out and what readers remember. There's a lot to unpack in this claim. Trust comes first. In turning off their filter, readers expect you to care for them. Contrast driving down a billboard filled street or doomscrolling past ads with reading your novel. The former has countless messages competing to break through the clutter. It's a battle to get anything remembered. Authors, conversely, contract to provide a calm space, an environment where words don't compete. In taking charge of this space, you implicitly commit to providing value. Putting out garbage, i.e. irrelevant detail, breaks that promise. The author / reader contract works backwards, as well. In selecting a detail to include, you alert readers to its significance and prompt them to remember it.

Before struggling over every word paralyzes you, remember reading is also somewhat holistic. Science can't describe exactly how reading works, except to say it qualitatively differs from direct experience (though it often has the same result, like simulacra.) Millenia of experience endorses doing all the things good writers do: optimal word selection, varied structure, vivid language and so on. At the same time, you need to think carefully about what information you disclose about your beings. The better you do at organizing your presentation, the more likely the right details will sink in, becoming part of the being the reader knows.

To probe the author / reader contract further, imagine you're on fire and need a friend to call 911. You don't run up, casually talk about the weather and scream fire (Google the hilarious I*T Crowd* scene). Trust, in the form of social convention, ensures this small talk doesn't precede an alarm. The unstated consensus is something so important comes first. Notice, also, how context flows through secondary channels in this and similar situations. If your clothes are burning, you don't have to say anything to get help. Writing shifts these expectations by placing the entire burden on the author's shoulders. Why? Because written works must always deliver context as well as plot. In other words, you have to provide backstory (the preamble) even as you describe your story's now (the fire).

Writing's unique, near simultaneous presentation of foreground and background fulfills two functions. Obviously, your words — first — set the stage, so readers can make sense of what's going on. The vivid language you use to describe a story's world, for instance, establishes a backdrop for your character's choices. Meanwhile, your words also spotlight the foreground and show readers what's important. Great authors tightly weave past and present together. In analyzing writing, however, it's helpful to separate the two. Understanding your need to deliver background as well as foreground underlines your duty to transmit effectively. Yes, simulacra have functionally unlimited space, but this capacity doesn't come close to guaranteeing whatever you write will stick. While they do pay reasonable attention, readers aren't cramming for a test. Their experience generally begins and ends with enjoying a story. The onus is on you to "teach" the necessary facts. Fulfilling this responsibility begins with figuring out what's relevant, cuing our long-awaited choosing the right seeds discussion.

Choose the Right Seeds to Plant

Picking seeds covers the supreme moment in your character's life — when readers meet them. Nearly all of this guide applies to this instant. To review, you know the desired outcome: accurate simulacrum formation, one that is both whole and matches the being in your mind. This process also doesn't take very long, either, a few seconds from start to finish. Next, you know how fragile introductions are. If readers don't "get" your character, you may not be able to correct the error. There are worse outcomes, as well. Readers may not recognize a character in what you write, a disaster which merits no further mention. And, finally, fostering investment is essential.

The seed metaphor aptly captures how to address these requirements and how to create the ideal intro. Seeds are small, connoting Minimum space. Next, a seed prefigures the plant to come, just as your intro must transfer your whole being, albeit in embryonic form. Most importantly, good gardeners pay close attention to planting. Don't picture a farmer scattering grain over a field. You get one seed, a single chance to make a first impression. In all, your seed must be carefully constructed. Then, the ground must be prepared. Finally, the kernel must be planted properly, sheltered and watered for it to germinate. With success, you move to cultivation in this guide's last chapter.

Naturally, your planting — the kickoff of the reader-character relationship — should be artful, particularly not confusing or boring. In addition, it requires worthy transitions to contextualize their entrance and maintain overall coherence. Let's skip those requirements to concentrate on the seed's contents. Put another way, the overriding objective is to choose what facts to transmit. In choosing facts, remember that you have a few paragraphs, probably less, to complete the introduction. Thus, you must view the introduction through the lens of salience.

Controlling Your Readers

Novelists, broadly speaking, have only three choices, your novel's symbolic control panel. First, you select their words. Curating language, for many, is the fun part. When anyone compliments your "beautiful" writing, a smile rises from your soul to renew your commitment to the craft. Yet, arguably, it's not the ultimate accolade and certainly not correlated with commercial success (to your chagrin, right?). Better to hear "great story" — the reaction that truly leads to fame and fortune. The takeaway, here, is a story's quality depends on more than word choice. So, what do authors do besides choose words? Two things: deciding how to order your words and decide how much to say about something. In short, you choose the sequence and the volume as well as what you say. These three choices, in turn, dictate the reading experience.

The importance of your words' sequence seems clear though often overlooked. Ordering affects your novel at every level. Microscopically, you arrange words and phrases in sentences. At the other extreme, you arrange sections and chapters. Order also operates more abstractly as you construct your story. You must organize your plot, for instance. Take some time to ponder sequencing's import.

If you need help, consider ordering's effects. Research and common sense follow a simple rule: what comes first is the most important. Primacy, this phenomenon's technical label, describes how we remember what comes first and how it shapes what comes after. This effect essentially generalizes the first impression phenomenon. Ordering also concerns what comes second, third and so on — all the way to what comes last. Speaking of coming last, "recency" is the technical term for a similar idea; it describes how we remember conclusions better than middles. Know that recency is a much weaker effect than primacy. Things we hear last tend to be top of mind for a bit, then fade.

Second: Sequencing, Including the Detail Ranking Exercise

The main lesson is presentation order, i.e. sequencing, largely governs what makes it into readers' memory. To apply this lesson, you need to prioritize your character's details. If this sounds weird, ask yourself what is the most important thing about my creature? This question, of course, assumes importance is a function of your story. It's also a better way to address relevance. Many take relevance to be an either/or binary choice; something is relevant or isn't. Importance, in our sense, is a more precise ranking. Your task, then, is to rank your character's details in order of story priority. For example, something readers absolutely must know about a character (to get the story) receives a one, placing it at the top. Consciously doing this exercise is vital to making a successful first impression.

You might ignore this ranking exercise and hope it happens automatically. In other words, your brain will figure out the important facts as you write. It won't. Why? Because you're already grokking your being holistically — satisfying Chapter Six's integration goal. Ordering your presentation, choosing what to pack into your seeds, poses another, completely separate challenge. In introducing your being, you move away from creation to transmission. It's very different. Planting seeds transfers the formed being to your readers. Were we telepathic, this would be easy. Instead, we're cursed (or blessed) with writing's slow, serial bandwidth. So, choosing seeds follows from identity construction, yet needs to be approached separately. Think of it like this: the construction task is yours and more independent while the transmission task has to account for readers and story.

Ranking each detail's significance is a prerequisite to effective transfers. It's very easy to mess up ranking, to fail to see the trees in the forest; in this case, to put the critical trees first. By not thinking about what's important, you tend to write what's available. In other words, recency dominates. Absent hard work, your latest thought, probably a change or embellishment, flows to the page. That's bad. To synergize readers and story with your introduction, you have to think extremely carefully about what's vital, what the reader must know to recreate the story. From the opposite angle, we only care about the facts whose absence would leave the reader lost. The end of this section unveils the gossip text — a way to rank the details well.

Third: Volume

Volume is a third choice; you decide how many words to spend on each detail. This seems equally obvious and is likewise oft ignored. The rule here is proportionality, or volume equals salience. Scientifically speaking, the more words you spend on a given detail, the more significant it is to readers. The things you write about most are what they'll remember. Again, it's a choice. Take that old reliable hair (or feet for Quentin Tarantino). Naive authors may wax on about a character's flowing locks, never failing to bring them up time and again. Pop quiz: name a being whose identity justifies this salience? Answer: Samson. One haircut and he loses everything. Stepping back, hair's centrality to him and to the story makes allocating these words the right choice. Proportionality governs salience because you're on a budget. A novel's limited word count forces you to think about whether each thing you might add — backstory in this case — is worthwhile. In turn, words spent signals how important a detail is. Readers tend to remember the aspects with the most words.

Start with a Name to Make It Easy for Readers

It's always wise to see yourself as part of the customer service industry. Rule one: treat your reader / customers well. With respect to introductions, know that we recognize others best when they have a name. Yes, it's conventional and obvious. On the other hand, there's a reason for names; for one, the character simulacrum stored in the reader's memory gets a label whether you supply one or not. Names have a function. Recall, i.e. pulling someone from memory, involves finding this label, for example. You remember the firefighter, for instance? Yes, his name is Pat! I know him. Hence the advice, share your creature's name ASAP.

You don't have to heed this (or any) advice; however, have a solid reason to ignore this fundamental. Weigh a heightened sense of mystery or drama, for instance, against readers not recognizing a main character. Naive authors also tend to mix up their star's names. They, for instance, use first name, last name and nickname interchangeably, making readers less than perfectly content. Be kind. You know they refer to the same being; they don't — at least not yet. Your audience can figure it out, probably, but why make them? Readers' energy and attention are better spent elsewhere. If you can't think of anything clever, go with this basic: a name that's used throughout the novel, then any nickname or other identifiers (like Captain) firmly attached.

A Good Name and Image

It goes without saying that the name itself should meet our criteria. First, it should be contextually plausible. Strive to make it interesting and meaningful, as well.

Coming up with a brilliant sobriquet, like Hiro Protagonist of *Snow Crash*, may be asking too much; coming up with an additive name — one which suits your being's identity — is a worthy goal. Finally, it should be mildly unique. An original name tends to be more memorable; moreover, a google amenable term gives future fame and fortune a tiny boost.

The next thing to hand over is a nascent mental image. Nearly all simulacra have a picture attached, a mental JPEG that helps us know the person. It makes sense. We use simulacra to recognize the beings they reference. The image your first impression conveys shouldn't be overdone, no more than a sentence. It's tempting to go farther. Perhaps you provide an extensive description of their luxurious wardrobe, something befitting royalty. For Pat, we could convey an image of him fully geared to fight fire, reaching hundreds of words. Know that, once again, it's about choices; words spent on clothes can't be spent elsewhere. Will readers find meaning, distraction or indulgence? Decide these things on a case by case basis to suit your story. More guidance follows under the "Gossip Test" heading. This said, meet the minimum unless you earn a waiver: a name and some physicality to establish the portrait you and your reader share.

Select a Now to Divide Past from Present

All fictional character's lives begin en media res, which is Latin for in the midst of things. As psychological studies that address human concerns, they can do nothing else. This necessity means you need to think about and set your being's timeframe. More specifically, you have to share your being's perspective on when the introduction takes place with your readers. This point in time also separates your creatures' past from their present. Moreover, that moment literally begins their life insofar as readers are concerned. Yes, it's really important. So, when should your character's story start?

Let's think about some extremes. You could, perhaps, imagine a common backstory for every fictional being. It would start with the big bang, at the universe's beginning, and proceed through Earth's formation to early humans. It's probably too much (unless you're Douglas Adams or Monty Python). Shifting frames to your character, you could start with their zygote — or alien facsimile —

the single cell from which a being genetically emerges. Indeed, some novels start at conception: *The Unconsoled, The House of the Spirits* or *The God of Small Things.* You could also pull a reverse and begin at death. This alternate commonality appears in *The Lovely Bones, The Death of Ivan Ilyich* and *The Book Thief.* Thus, a table laden with these options, everything in between and more sits before you. Put another way, you — the auteur — get to decide where to set your being's point of departure. Only the need to embed their story in human experience constrains your choices.

What does setting a departure point do; what is its function? Put simply, it divides your being's arc into past and present. Readers are extraordinarily sensitive to timing. Their desire to make sense of your story drives a demand to pin down your story's now. (In this sense, "now" doesn't mean a historical era.) So, with the usual caveats, you should timestamp your character's present at introduction. This stamp orients your readers to the character's life. It gives them the perspective to distinguish past, present and future. After orientation, readers more or less automatically follow your timeline, and store any new information accordingly. Absent a baseline for this clock, things get mushy fast. A fix on their present is absolutely necessary for effective flashbacks, for one. Of course, this technique is an excellent way to deliver backstory.

Pick any point in your being's life to apply this thought. Everything before this line is history, and everything after is story. In this way, your introduction's content falls into two categories: backstory and now. Notice how this distinction matches the identity-backstory separation. Identity is now; backstory isn't. Explicitly adding a timestamp facilitates orienting the reader properly. In this way, it supports storytelling going forward, so long as you lovingly tend to your readers' ability to track your creature's timeline with respect to this moment.

The Gossip Test for Backstory

Pragmatically, your character's life begins when readers meet them. Hence, their history conducts them to this time and place. Let's modify this point slightly: an introduction must include history sufficient (and barely more) to describe what brought your being to that point in the story. Your introduction also has to launch their relationship with your reader, both quickly and effectively. Think small space, big impact. And, of course, it must be contextualized. As your story sets the context, aim to provide enough of the right details. All this implies introductions should be seen as tight packages of details. The need to respect Goldilocks bears repeating. The package can't be too big or too small, and everything inside this package must be just right, i.e. relevant. The word, relevance, appears over and over because it's so important; it drives the ranking task described above, for instance. How can we address these two needs, for sufficiency and relevance?

The indispensable tool comes from our social lives; this technique is so powerful, it's almost a secret weapon. It's called gossip. Like stereotypes, gossip gets a bad rap; like stereotypes, don't let this vilification stand in the way of using it to move you toward winning a reader's love. This section, hopefully, devotes enough words for you to award this amazing, yet universal, ability the salience it merits. Then, use gossip to rank what to say about your being.

Gossip's Utility

First and foremost, gossip is inherently social. An isolated human never gossips, imaginary friends excepted. (This way to deal with isolation highlights gossip's value.) Wherever a group forms, gossip erupts; as groups grow, the opportunities to gossip expand rapidly. It takes three people to gossip; two get to talk about the other one, giving three opportunities. With six people, there are 15 opportunities — probably more.

Gossip's importance increases as our social groups grow even larger. Past some point, witnessing everyone's actions directly becomes impossible. Researchers' theory of gossip suggests it fosters our species' survival. One sign of this evolutionary utility is that an unexpectedly large area of our prefrontal cortex — the "pleasure" center if you will — lights up when we engage in this allegedly unsavory practice. In other words, we enjoy gossip and benefit from it, disdainfully or not.

Gossip benefits individuals as well as groups. It offers individuals insight, not least into others' goals and behaviors. Reputations summarize these insights. For example, a gossip might warn against loaning your stone to Ug; he doesn't return them. This social practice helps us pick people to trust. Engaging in gossip also strengthens relationships among the sharers, particularly if the information seems beneficial. Giving someone a juicy tidbit encourages reciprocity and common perspective, bringing you closer. From the group's perspective, gossiping knits people together. A friend of a friend is more likely to be friendly. Similarly, knowing a bit about someone new accelerates the friendship. For example, avoid this topic, i.e. don't bring up Ug's rock hoarding. It can also help heal existing rifts. Ug feels really bad about his obsession, go talk to him. Finally, forming a gossip network promotes norms and cohesion. Ug knows he's getting a bad rep, which pushes him toward doing the right thing and returning the stones. These little gains add up to a functioning society.

Unsurprisingly, gossip appears everywhere anthropologists observe. These studies also show gossip tends to be balanced, not malicious, which is what you'd expect for it to be useful. Long before social media, we passed the time talking about others. Meanwhile, gossip is entertaining; it has to be to capture the audience's attention. Successful gossip follows the viral social media formula. What's the key word? Relevance, of course. A good gossip knows their audience and what they want (and need) to hear. Only then do secondary factors, like pacing and voice, come to the fore. Authors, keen observers that you are, should readily spot its role in social bonding and productive group dynamics. You should also witness the reward talented gossips accrue; they win attention even as they cement a central position in their social network. The combination of utility and pleasure make gossip irresistible despite any injunction.

Use Gossip to Write

Why is this important for you? Gossip is a noun and a verb, a kind of information as well as its distribution. Each sense can contribute to setting up your intro. Gossip the noun conveys needed social information quickly and entertainingly. From this perspective, hot goss fills in the details piece by piece, granting understanding and encouraging empathy. Each bit concerns a specific human, passed along mostly informally while being exceedingly memorable. Common topics include relationships, social status, achievements and failures. This content attempts to explain the whys behind the target's behavior. Along with facts, gossip the verb fosters mutuality. Discussing others' challenges offers perspective in addition to empowerment, relief or both. Finally, gossip's violation of privacy can actually bring the hearer closer to the source and into a trusted circle. Providing inside information, for instance, builds trust between you and your readers.

The approbation gossip attracts flows from its reliance on private or sensational details. It also connotes a less savory locale, i.e. behind the subject's back. It assuredly has negative effects, especially on the subject's trust. Paraphrasing the Google warning's: recognize its potential harms and use it responsibly. Thanks, Google! Your being is fictional, so let's not worry about their feelings too much — done. That said, having characters gossip about other characters raises interesting issues, which Chapter Eight addresses. Overall, then, gossips are nosy, backbiting liars. Time to slap them? No, time to join them.

Use your innate talent for gossip to construct backstory and select the facts your intro delivers. As always, the key is relevance. So, imagine yourself at a party — one set in your story. You and your reader sit together, above the action, just as a new character pops in. Now, you have a few sentences, to bring the reader up to speed before they engage. So, who is this guy? You only get a few behind the back whispers to set the stage for their interaction. The gossip test pinpoints their contextual essence and helps you select the relevant seeds.

Dynamic Necessity

The concept of dynamic necessity holds that a story's context determines how much you have to say at any point in your story; namely you must satisfy the reader's instant curiosity. It's an antidote to confusion. You should write just enough for the reader to move on. It's also an antidote to boredom, which keeps you from saying too much. In terms of dynamic necessity, an introduction has to satisfy the reader, so they feel like they know your being. More precisely, you need to provide enough details to temporarily answer every obvious question. Skillful authors almost instinctively know what and how much to say. With practice, you will too.

So, what exactly do you write? Only the critical facts, like Joe Friday for the aged (Google). Why, for instance, did they show up at this moment? Then, mix in the one or two most important things about them. More often than not, this data concerns your being's motivation as well as the situation they face. The point of view matters but not as much as you may think. An unreliable narrator can do the job as well as an omniscient one. The info in this detail package only needs to suit the context; it has to be dynamically necessary. Following this guide's advice, it's not an exhaustive backstory, just a simulacrum's seeds.

Think of gossip as an opening social media post or a news summary. A quick rundown to capture the reader's attention and start the empathy ball rolling. Keep it interesting, essential and brief. Naturally, you should use the one or two things from the top of the ranking exercise. You did it right? Double check your ranking to see that your gossip only contains situationally vital information. At the moment of meeting, it takes surprisingly little to satisfy the reader's need to know what they are all about.

Testing Your Intro

The retelling test works particularly well here. Hand the beta reader the chapter with a main character's introduction and see what sticks in their memory. It should, needless to say, match the highest ranked details in your exercise. If not, there's work to be done. Now, apply the caveats regarding juggling and coherence to ensure that the being introduced aligns with the being who appears throughout the story. Like every test, you should also look for enthusiasm. You want your reader to demonstrate an interest in your creation (from the situational or dispositional factors described earlier). Do they want to get to know your being better? The answer better be yes.

In all, a *publishable* character's seeding requires three things. First, provide a sufficient name and a short sketch of salient, distinguishing physical features. Second, supply the dynamically necessary reason for them to appear at this point. Third, give one or two (rarely three) key facts. You're aiming for a smooth yet satisfying beginning; you want to spin up simulation accurately while harnessing your reader's interest. Writing more than a long paragraph signals danger. This can't be an info dump. Remember Zeus, who pushed our Athena in her entirety? You're not him. The aptness of this Greek God metaphor stems from the identity work you've done. Your being should be close to fully formed after you follow those instructions. However, choosing seeds separates transmission from creation. Put another way, you must select part of your creature to share.

Planting these seeds provides a foundation, nothing more. You have the rest of your story to nurture them. Their growth, which is a result of your character's choices, literally brings them to life. Then, empathy builds as the reader's simulacrum expands to match yours, drawing you closer to earning your reader's love.

Chapter 08

Agency: Build Their Lives in Your Story

Publishability Index™ Goals:

(Good) Characters reveal themselves through thoughts and choices

(Great) Understandable and cumulative change emerges from their behavior

PREVIEW

1. Character choice is central as it demonstrates agency and produces empathy (via the Golden Chain).

2. This chain is a set of mental processes that turn your words into empathy when you provide sufficient info, which prompts readers to make predictions and to consider how they themselves would act

3. The chain ends when readers witness your character's choice; then, the immediate consequence seals the vicarious experience. In this way, the reader's mind brings your beings to life.

4. Readers learn, i.e. update their simulacra, from inaccurately predicting your being's choices.

5. Successful plotting demands coherently linking choice situations and structuring learning to create a character arc.

6. It's good to have three main characters.

7. Putting identity first means your being's actions, including dialogue, will emerge organically from the context, including other characters, and lead to deep empathy.

By now you've properly introduced a potential fan to your character. If you haven't taken time to appreciate this god level achievement, do so. Surpassing Dr. Frankenstein and his patched together creature, you've birthed an integrated entity who's as relatable as most humans. Mary Shelley's tale investigates humanity; your tale, more than likely, can take that gift for granted. So, pat yourself on the back, and let's move on to consider your creature's current, perilous state.

While it may seem time to let them loose, release them into the wild and so on, hold your horses. These metaphors inspire but fail to bring attention to the mandatory next step. Recall that your abiogenic being originates in hijacking the faculties readers use for everyday people. This mental process generates a constructed life from the words you put into their heads. Yet, this mental model, an identity with suitable backstory, is a parasite. It lives through your reader's time and energy and has provided little in return to this point. They require further investment to sustain them, let alone to grow and prompt empathy. To prevent their untimely end, you have to reward the reader regularly (and pay a giant lump sum at the end).

Empathy, Arcs and Success Follows Choice

Chapter Three discussed general motives for reading; here, more granularity is required. What will keep your greedy reader loanshark from breaking your legs, i.e. DNF? Less colorfully, what encourages them as they recreate your story? The answer is vicariously experiencing your creature's choices and to jointly make worthwhile decisions where possible. This premise is an oversimplification which serves a purpose. It orients your efforts to a singular necessity. This focus should dictate how you spend words. It also pulls in associated concepts, like goals and agency, as well as outcomes, like growth and change. You don't have to concentrate on choice; however, know that readers' recreations of your story will always revolve around your character's decisions. It's part of the way humans understand stories and what they teach about behavior. The endless quest to make sense of others' actions — places choice at a novel's heart, intentionally or otherwise.

Fictional life balances on agency due to the primacy of choice. The word balance deliberately replaces something like foundation, which implies agency remains strong once built. Balance, in contrast, connotes the precariousness of your imitation's existence, especially the illusion of free will; it's always prone to toppling off and crashing. Put another way, agency is fleeting and needs constant reinforcement. Naturally, you've heard of agency and its importance. If you haven't, it's the ability to make choices or otherwise act independently. In fiction, agency, along with illusory free will, comes from the working of your being's corresponding simulation. Recall simulacra primarily help us forecast other humans' behavior, answering the question what will they do? They serve the same purpose for readers with respect to your creature. To experience a character's life vicariously means figuring out potential actions and consequences, then predicting one and checking it against what your creation actually does. In performing these actions, the reader's mind brings your character to life.

Cultivating Empathy

Your main task, given this focus on choice, is to provide information. Your audience has to get what's going on; put another way, they have to understand (and so be able to place themselves within) the choice situation. So, what must readers know? Everything needed to make and check a prediction. Underline the word prediction; making a prediction concerning what your character will do is the primary act on the road to empathy. The information you must provide about each choice includes available options, situational factors and likely consequences. In forecasting, either thoughtfully or automatically, a reader takes this info and feeds it into the corresponding person model. Then that simulacrum sifts through alternatives to pick the best from the character's perspective.

Notice, this forecast doesn't have to be perfect; in fact you can take advantage of "bad" predictions. This complex topic will take several of this guide's sections to cover. To preview: first, right or wrong doesn't matter in terms of the thrill and immediate empathy, which comes from the act of predicting. Second, the prediction's accuracy is important when it comes to one of two possibilities, either grokking or learning. An accurate forecast indicates progress toward deep empathy (that wonderful state where reader and creature are of one mind) because the reader's decisions synchronize with the character's. That said, an inaccurate forecast is perfectly fine, as well, because it leads to learning. When the reader sees their model's prediction could have been better, they improve the simulacrum in a process called updating. In other words, a "bad" prediction leads to them knowing more about your being. Finally — and this is a lot to layer on, you must eventually produce a character arc by controlling your audience's updates.

The main lesson lurks behind these processes: empathy comes from continually setting up story productive choices. You know this task (roughly) as plotting. To preview, again, it's not an exaggeration to believe stories fall into two parts. One hand offers the available choices while the other contextualizes them. Expanding on choice, keep in mind your carefully constructed story supplies the environment in which your *publishable* character lives. Thus, your story has to deliver the context that sets up choice situations. At the same time, it has to deliver the investable identity of the being making the choices. Putting identity and situations together allows your creation to live through the simulated actions they take. This guide's section after the next examines how to construct and sequence these events, with an eye toward maximizing empathy, in discussing the Golden Chain.

Agency Builds From The Illusion of Free Will

The empathy process begins when a significant choice confronts your character. Before diving in, a dash of philosophy may ground this claim. Metaphysicians' (and Monty Python's) root questions concern life and its meeting. What's it all about, they ask. Our sufficient answer, unsurprisingly, is choice. This simple act, selecting between two or more actions, troubles scientists as well as philosophers. The so-called problem of free will fruitfully encapsulates the debate. On one side, people argue prior causes govern every action; put starkly, they believe humans aren't autonomous. B. F. Skinner gained fame for an extreme stimulus-response behaviorism; he claimed our choices are entirely reactive and come from learned reinforcements. Plants, for example, turn toward the sun to get energy; to him, human behavior boils down to a complicated version of this reflex. The other side believes in genuine choice. This translates to explaining behavior in terms of goals and intentions. Note, not every decision has to be thoughtful to be autonomous. Jurgen Habermas suggests such deliberation rarely happens; though it represents our best selves, we often motor on in life on autopilot, automatically choosing the best option without much thought.

Good storytelling forces authors to respect the genuine choice view. Of course, your being's free will is illusory because you author, forgive the pun, their actions. Nevertheless, writing a novel isn't compatible with believing in a deterministic world. There may be irony in someone lacking free will reading about a fictional being, who pretends to have it. (Maybe that would make a great story.) Back to the point: readers must witness your character's agency for them to be authentic and investable. To illustrate, imagine writing a purely reactive creation. Events, good or bad, toss them around. They bounce from one situation to the next like rubber balls or punching bags. These caricatures may win sympathy as they endure their author's torture, but pity isn't enough for a satisfying story. All characters are the author's puppets; however, it takes the magic of pretend agency to turn them into relatable beings.

Publishable characters should radiate autonomy. They observe and take action — always, always choosing. Free will manifests through their inner dialogue as they struggle over what to do. It also appears in their conversations with others. Further, the scenarios you construct must have — genre consistent — stakes for the reader to care. In this vein, an easy choice is no choice at all; a difficult decision, conversely, clarifies everything. It takes a grave dilemma, one with no good options, to really get your audience's juices flowing.

Respecting the Golden Chain Leads to Empathy

Given everything we know about how readers use simulacra to relate to your beings, it should surprise you that they are critical to developing empathy. Without too much exaggeration, then, achieving empathy demands nurturing your character's corresponding simulacrum. It's your main task largely because readers' brains do the rest; specifically, their complicated chain of mental processes turn your words into knowledge and emotion. Notice, this work goes on inside their heads; this means you can't directly control what they do. You only control the words which go into this chain. Let's take a closer look and go over this chain's consequences.

From Reading to Empathy

Science provides loose but extremely useful insight into how empathy works. The following path, which we'll call the Golden Chain, describes how a reader's mind responds to your words. Initially, it processes the words, picking out and forwarding choice situations to the appropriate simulacrum. Next, this model instantly predicts the course of action the character is likely to follow. Generating this prediction also seems to compel readers to make a parallel choice — what they themselves would do when faced with the same challenge. The magic of vicariousness ensues. Then, the brain observes the character's selection. When the character's decision confirms the prediction, confidence in the model goes up. Put simply, the reader feels they know the character better. Otherwise — when the prediction doesn't match — the model updates, i.e. the reader learns about the character. (Note, this inaccuracy doesn't refer to unreliable narrators, misdirection or other literary devices; rather, it refers to simple mistakes. For example, I thought they would do this, but they did that.) Finally, the reader can also analyze the decision, which may occur much later, looking to assign responsibility and draw lessons about your being, i.e. update, and more generally.

The Golden Chain's distillation of reading is still far more complicated than many authors would wish. Here's the key: the story has to go through a character's entire decision loop. This includes the consequences, especially the immediate impact of a choice. Absent some instant consequence, the energy invested in the choice dissipates. Thus, the progress you're making on the road toward empathy vanishes, and the gap between reader and your being grows wider. The opportunities to heighten familiarity or to learn also disappear. Naturally, detailing the immediate result represents the bare minimum of what you should offer. The aim is to let readers savor and cement the vicarious experience. Remember every decision should have effects which reverberate through the novel. A proper inciting incident, for example, includes a decision that affects what follows.

To illustrate, let's imagine a friend asks Pat to help cheat on an exam. The options — yes, no or maybe — have a multitude of stakes attached to each. The reader's mind will send this situation to their Pat model and await an answer. If the scenario makes sense, i.e. the options and likely outcomes are cognizable, the simulacrum responds with a prediction. This output stems from everything the reader knows about Pat, both directly from the writing as well as anything added in Co-Creation, as well as the context. As this happens, the reader also decides how they would react themselves. The parallel decision making — one simulated by the model and one imagined by the reader — engenders empathy.

Next, the outcome, Pat's choice, is read. Readers absolutely have to observe this decision; seeing your being's actual choice lets them assess their prediction's accuracy. In turn, this comparison allows for increased comfort or learning. They have to know what Pat did, even if it was just some kind of delay. What happened isn't that important in terms of empathy. The empathy chain, instead, focuses on the model's accuracy. The essential issue is how well it captures Pat. So, the reader's brain compares their prediction to what Pat did. A correct prediction confirms their Pat knowledge. Pat behaved as expected; the model works. Inaccuracy, an "out-of-character" selection (again, not unreliability or intentional misdirection), shows the Pat model needs improvement. So, they "fix" the model accordingly. Pat becomes more or less moral, puts a higher or lower emphasis on friendship and so on. The reader can also compare what they would have done. More on this possibility momentarily.

The lesson to takeaway is the reader then must feel some immediate consequence to provoke empathy. Depending on the story, Pat's decision will have a greater or lesser impact. Here, the concern is timing. The reader's mind wants and waits for closure before moving on. This direct impact doesn't have to be a big deal, but it has to be something. Emotions are a good candidate for the instantaneous aftermath; they use inner monologue to bypass the reader's filter and lead directly to vicariousness. Consider the "curses, foiled again" trope. This expression manifests the villain's failure while letting the audience empathize and move on. In Pat's case, imagine and artfully describe the emotional state that accompanies the choice. For example, a sigh suggests resignation; guilt, anger or joy offer other avenues to explore. Overall, satisfaction comes from staying with Pat through the moment and after, until reading about how the being "felt" seals the deal.

Let's tie the Golden Chain to the purpose of reading and the possibilities it offers. Simulacra accept the wildest situations even as your being's identity stays relatively static. Reality, hence, plays little part in turning the choices set up into predictions. In other words, you can drop your being anywhere in space or time and excerpt them to react accordingly. For example, *Sense and Sensibility's* Marianne Dashwood could wake up in contemporary New York and order breakfast after an initial shock. With motivation, the brain goes a step further; it plays around with variations in an attempt to get at what's going on, to find meaning. Continuing the Pat cheating illustration, they imagine what might happen if the bribe went up to $50,000. Would that make a difference to the character and to the reader? Their thinking could involve multiple threads. One line of inquiry, for example, concerns the reward; does money make it more heinous? What about a million? What if Pat is starving or blackmailed? Once activated, the reader's mind interrogates the simulacrum, tracing through the facts like a prosecutor to make a judgment and find meaning in Pat's actual decision.

What's more, their investigation into any character's behavior follows the author's lead. Entire novels, like *The Count of Monte Cristo*, have been devoted to driving the reader to the verdict the author wants. You may call this the theme. Differences between readers, especially across locations and times, amplify this creative challenge. Nevertheless, we're certain we would have done exactly what Edmond Dantès did (and would have suffered the same fate) hundreds of years later. Never understate Alexandre Dumas' (or his fellows') accomplishment. You don't have to reach these heights to be successful, but you must orchestrate your words through the entire Golden Chain, the mental processes that turn words into empathy, every time your being makes a choice to achieve any lasting impact.

Show Don't Tell

This conclusion regarding empathy lends itself to the "show don't tell" wisdom. In short, this dicta commands you to avoid bluntly stating things in favor of allowing your audience to recognize them via dialogue or action. It's fantastic advice. Right away, it produces more interesting writing because it resembles life more closely. Few people wander around loudly proclaiming their emotional state. Moreover, they rarely say such things to themselves. No healthy person displays the self-absorption some lengthy (read boring) inner monologues require. In short, inner thoughts should not be used as a bullhorn. Show don't tell, more subtly, also increases the reader's burden. Wait a minute: increase the burden? Yes, in this way: we naturally infer emotional and other states. You wouldn't think twice if Pat announces "I'm hungry" but hearing "I feel a deep-seated need to eat to make up for a lack of parental love" gives pause. In reading, your audience happily applies these skills without noticing the effort. Doing so, thus, feeds their investment.

Your Responsibility: Orchestrating Everything

Time to round out our description of your authorial duties; specifically, to add the Golden Chain's implications. Recall brains treat anything resembling an autonomous being as a real person. Thus, simulacra can easily capture literally fantastic beings. Let's touch on how far out things can get. Say Pat is actually a magic-using, intelligent dragon in disguise. It's wild but still plausible. They also admit equally fantastic scenarios. Perhaps Pat comes from a future where dragons fight a last stand against a mutli-universal nano particle hive mind. Like *Don Quixote*, this scenario turns what seems like a search for a fire hydrant into unlocking a transdimensional portal. Pause to see if you can dream up something more outlandish. Unless you find such speculation repellent, your brain can digest almost any scenario. More to the point, you can find a bit of empathy for Pat no matter how much the context diverges from our lives.

Reading a *publishable* character's adventures takes over the brain so well that reality's constraints disappear. Recall Chapter Three explained how existence grants real people automatic authenticity. Similarly, human history mostly coheres because it actually happened. Even there, however, substantial effort goes into turning a historical incident into a good story. Reality, for example, isn't enough to make a crime story compelling although it may come straight from news reports. Common events, like a family reunion, demand a commensurate interpretation. Think through this task. Constructing a story demands collecting facts, piecing them together and trying to produce a sensible narrative. As hard as it seems, there's more. Understanding itself is slippery; theorists call it contingent, partial and limited. Note, this observation applies to any genre. Don't dwell on this point; instead, remember this lesson: an arduous, crooked path leads from real life to a good story.

To plunge further down this rabbit hole, consider how novels — via the GC — insist readers repeatedly judge a main character's actions. Would your audience blame Pat should a firefighting teammate die? This question could be the prelude to a complicated adjudication, one that mirrors a murder trial. Imagine your reader's verdict as the outcome of a lengthy legal proceedings. There's an investigation, testimony with cross-examination, expensive lawyers and a wizened judge. Then, a jury tromps back into the reader's mental courtroom. Guilty! Or, innocent; it doesn't matter (so long as you maintain coherence) so long as the reader is invested. There's more. Real juries go home. The reader, in contrast, sifts the verdict for lessons as they move to the next point in Pat's story. Vicarious experience also makes them an accessory to any crime, which reinforces its impact. Finally, at a completely different level, readers know that the author hides behind every word, pulling strings.

What role do you really play in all this? Orchestration. This imperative appeared earlier; here, it solidifies into actionable advice. Put simply: you must establish and maintain coherence while building situations that achieve empathy. Recall you have three controls (detailed in Chapter Seven) to arrange: selecting words, sequencing them and their volume. The desired outcome is equally clear: a satisfied reader. Understanding empathy adds another layer which realizes the plant metaphor. You prepare the ground, then water and fertilize the simulacrum nested in the reader's mind. This nurturing gives life to your being. Thus, while events ostensibly occur on the page, they're actually experienced by the reader as well as their model of your character. Inner dialogue, for example, flows over the reader's filter smack into the simulation as more facts for it to ingest. In so doing, the model maintains itself, especially its illusory autonomy, and expands.

The investment retelling test highlights how to effectively orchestrate your words. For a given choice, or plot point, any reader / volunteer should be able to list the options. They should also be able to describe the context; more precisely, they should restate the background necessary to make a prediction — give the character's identity — in their own words. Notice, these details also feed into the reader's simultaneous choice as to which option they themselves would pick. Effectively orchestrating your words, then, demands transferring these details, as a package, to the reader. It also demands not going overboard. You must avoid overcomplication, info dumping and heavy-handedness in favor of coherent transmission. Keep authenticity in mind, as well. Examine the possibilities and actions to ensure their contextual realism. In short, use a light touch, convey just enough so the reader can pass the test. Recall that the test looks for the prediction; making it, along with experiencing consequences, puts readers into your character's head (and vice versa).

Recognize Your Being's Goals

Writing advice unanimously stresses the importance of goals, motivations and the like. This guide unequivocally endorses this view. We won't spend much time on their import, save to point out their role in the Golden Chain. This critical application occurs at crossroads where your character chooses what to do. In short, what your being wants drives choice. Their objectives produce movement, which the illusion of autonomy elevates to an intention. Or course, intentions walk hand in hand with agency. Goalless creatures are inert and lack agency, by definition, because they don't do anything. Not only are such beings boring, they can't provoke empathy. Reread the last few pages if you disagree. Desire is also absolutely necessary for conflict, the wellspring of drama.

Identity Still Comes First

Given the importance writing advice gives goals, you'd be forgiven for thinking they lead character creation. No! Your character's desires, like backstory, must come from identity. Rehearse our motto; identity comes first, last and always. Hence, it falls to you to examine your being and find out what motivates them. Only this fosters actions that align with and extend identity. Again, out-of-character behavior subverts authenticity. You're able to eliminate this danger through careful orchestration. Deploy the retelling test to eliminate any doubts. Should a volunteer fail to include your being's aims in their first pass, probe for them. Ask: what do they, insert name, want? Like the Spice Girls, the answer should come back loud and clear. Trust the Character Equation by looking at the way its three sources: yourself, cultural knowledge — in the form of stereotypes — and the distinctiveness stolen from referents feed into your creature. You may want to have more interactions, as well to address issues, such as a lack of clarity, during revision. Overall, knowing your being — having a well-integrated and sufficiently detailed model of them — makes ascertaining their wants straightforward.

Intentionality's Contribution

That said, it's vital to clearly specify your character's goals. Let's return to acting school, courtesy of Konstantin Stanislavski, for emphasis. Visit any set and you'll hear actors and directors huddle over characters. The word "intention" pops up over and over. Why? Intentions — the mind's orientation toward an objective — bridge wants and action. Stanislavski and acolytes developed this idea into an acting method, their "system" for lifelike performances. Chapter Seven dismissed one part, extensive backstory, as counterproductive to writing novels; however, his foundational idea is enlightening. In other words, the premise works though the application differs. He taught that every action, including spoken lines, should display a clear intention. Recall audiences' ability to see actors means performances depend on controlling microexpressions. Having an intention at the top of mind helps. Hence, Stanislavski actors settle on a specific goal for their scenes. For example, someone seeking an escape would constantly glance at the door. The result is a more psychologically realistic portrayal. More broadly, this method demands actors thoroughly explore a character's motivations.

Injecting a healthy dose of intentionality, an orientation toward goals, works wonders for a novel's characters. Above all, it imbues them with purpose, which reinforces their agency. An intentional being is the opposite of inert. This mentality can also create action without movement. For instance, seeking revenge transforms sitting still into calculating when to strike. On screen audiences see this tension, perhaps a stare or a twitching finger, while writing conveys this energy through description and inner monologue. In both cases, elevating a desire brings the character to life. Take this lesson to heart: having intentions heightens authenticity, stokes emotion and, most importantly, enables choice. All the above expand the opportunities for empathy, but the last, making decisions, is an absolute necessity. The Golden Chain only works for intentional characters.

How Preferences Work

We often see our preferences as obvious and set in stone. We spend little time discussing or analyzing them. Economists spout the Latin phrase de gustibus non est disputandum, which translates to there is no disputing taste. Less jargony, people like what they like, so leave it be. Pat hates chocolate but loves strawberry ice cream. Maybe it's weird. Who hates chocolate? Or, maybe you prefer the opposite. It's not important; hand over the strawberry. This approach works to a point; however, it breaks down in the face of more complicated issues. Refer back to one sticky situation, should Pat assist a cheater? Economists resolve this issue by reducing human motivation to wanting money, which they disguise as "utility" maximization.

Authors don't have this luxury; you can't reduce a complicated character to a singular want. As you know, your reader won't empathize with beings who make one-dimensional, reactive choices. (This doesn't apply to minor characters.) Authenticity demands more; it calls for nuanced priorities that mirror human's everyday complexity. The availability of different desires is a great resource for authors. This truth about nuance also separates goals from backstory. A human's backstory is relatively set; objectives, in contrast, are dynamic. Our motivations change from situation to situation and over time. The same pattern applies to your characters. Pragmatically speaking, your story reveals a static backstory; on the other hand, pinpointing a singular want for a main character should be impossible.

The rule is goals reflect identity as well as circumstances. Recall identity is situationally dependent; changing contexts brings different aspects of our multifaceted identity to the fore. Because desire stems from identity, it responds to situations, too. It may seem unintuitive. Think of it this way: the context helps frame an identity to isolate exactly what aspect and goal applies to the choice. Remember that you can't draw an aspect of identity at random; you must consider the situation and figure out what part of identity it elevates. For example, a threatened child will bring out a protective parent. In short, knowing your being as well as their wants guides you toward which aspects apply in a given scene. This approach supports character integration and organic behavior, furthering authenticity.

Finally, high stakes decisions usually transform into a competition between identities. Two facets of identity, for example, arise in response to Pat's choice regarding helping a friend cheat. The moral Pat, on one shoulder, says "this isn't right" while the friendly Pat says "help him out" on the other. Don't mistake these for angels and devils. Be aware that the best version of these struggles deliver shades of gray. The proper construction ensures the reader's imaginary courtroom trial could go either way; hence, the dilemma. And, readers love this chance to vicariously experience your genre's flavor of complex, weighty decisions. Additionally, this kind of internal struggle supplies a substantial chunk of the conflict every novel needs, a topic outside this guide's scope.

Finding Nuanced Priorities

Like identity, a person's goals may seem to be well-organized. For example, a greedy person wants money, so they always choose the largest expected payout. Nothing could be further from the truth; a given human's desires are a mess, reflecting our complexity. Think of this mess as a resource; these internal clashes introduce productive conflict. There's a practical issue, as well. A broad desire has to be refined and narrowed before it applies to a circumstance's peculiarities. Realize that fruitful opportunities arise in matching objectives to a particular decision. We'll discuss situation construction in the penultimate section. Suffice to say, a great author constructs situations to develop their character. Moreover, successfully architecting choice situations requires inducing organic behavior; put another way, your being's choices must, as discussed, follow their identity. In short, you have to think your way toward authenticity. When you get stuck, and we all do, more interaction provides a way forward. Play therapist (or sensitive friend; they're less expensive), and talk through the choice; again, a puppet comes in handy. Ask it, what do you want? What are you afraid of? What do you expect will happen? Is this a pattern? Having used the Character Equation and its exercises, your puppet — a manifestation of your simulacrum — should answer. If they don't, work your way back and push until they do. They will. Simulacra are designed to do exactly this kind of scenario analysis. Not only will you discover a response; you'll also develop your character as a side benefit. Further, seize the opportunity to add interesting parts of these conversations to your novel. This (and testing) is a great way to ensure readers understand your being's actions. Most of the time, of course, you won't need the puppet; you can happily roll along writing organic action because you know your creation. Their situational wants won't be hard to discover once you've set up options and context.

Throw in some uncertainty for fun, i.e. investment. Perfection is boring, We make mistakes; we break down; options aren't clear, and so forth. Perfect transparency gets boring, anyway. Spice up the Golden Chain by making its factors, such as the options and the expected results, less obvious. It's more realistic, too. Choices rarely arrive in black and white. Further, we're rarely confident about what will happen after we make a choice. Thus, we may choose A over B based on a hunch rather than solid evidence. As if it weren't enough to obscure the future (from the character-reader's point of view), there are always unintended consequences. Everything may point to choosing A, yet this selection leads to disaster. In short, you're allowed to (and should) build situations that frustrate, or otherwise lead, your being to a new path. At another level, your character has to learn about themselves and grow, which brings us to the subject of arcs.

Guide Reader Learning to Produce Arcs

Novels are stories, so they need a beginning, middle and end. To obey this convention, your character needs an arc. Before talking about these trajectories, note the possible confusion between arcs, which curve, and knowledge, which increases in a fairly straight line. More precisely, knowledge, i.e. a simulacrum's detail, goes up as you feed in facts. Your reader, ideally, learns a few relevant items (already ranked right?) from each chapter. They add these details to the model, automatically embellishing as they do. Empathy depends on this growth. Moreover, by novel's end, they should know your creation as well as anyone they've actually met. It's important to plan ahead and / or look back to check your work. As you'd expect, it's a wonderful idea to use the retelling test. See how well you nurtured your character by assessing what a volunteer knows about and what they feel toward your character at the very end.

Arcs, in contrast to knowledge, don't follow a line. Like agency, let's begin discussing arcs with a philosophical query: do beings change? Maybe or maybe not, but only with respect to real humans. (So much for philosophy.) *Publishable* characters, however, must change. Some big change, a metamorphosis, an adjustment or a switch, must happen to maintain reader investment. Readers also expect to see some effect when looking back at your story. Don't disappoint them. This growth falls under the search for meaning which motivates their attention. And, it's fun. Recall inert creatures are boring, so you want your being to move, a movement that takes the form of an arc. Who can resist a stunning, albeit well planned, transformation? Thus, beyond radiating agency in the instant, your being has to grow and change over the course of the novel to really earn their imaginary life.

Arcs require the same careful orchestration as the other factors we've discussed. That said, they don't require as deep a look into the human mind to appreciate. Why? Because they take place over a longer time span. Recall, the Golden Chain describes empathy's origin in the process of reading. Arcs, in contrast, develop over the course of entire novels. Moreover, an arc's impact won't land until its end. Everything this guide has covered leads to two points. Let's state them succinctly before unpacking them. First, an arc emerges from the situations your character faces, their choices and the consequences they suffer. And, second, simulacra are where changes in a character's identity happen. Thus, to successfully orchestrate an arc, you must deliver words that prompt simulacrum refinements which, in turn, add up to the big change you plan.

To ensure authentic growth and change it has to be sensible at each point. (Moreover, it's hard to recover lost sensibility.) Thus, you build an arc through incremental changes in goals. These little alterations will accumulate and shift your being's identity. This approach works because readers readily accept that objectives change from one situation to the next. So, relatively small adjustments, which don't cross over to confusion, slide beneath an audience's radar. Meanwhile, readers use their simulacra to track your character's choices and adjust their model. Each change enters the simulacrum through a slightly unexpected choice. In other words, each time you alter your being's situational goal from what they would have done to doing something slightly different, you lead the model to the next version of the character. With care, the incremental changes pile up until they're noticed and transform your being. The idea is to let the arc creep up on readers until it lands with a sudden realization, a big bang.

It's a complicated process, so let's use our friend to illustrate. Make Pat a hothead, who regularly goes off the rails and gets into fights. The planned arc centers on learning to control their temper, so we want the reader to see a calmer being by the novel's end. (It's not Shakespeare.) We need to induce this change over the course of thirty or so steps. Further, readers find sporadic growth, which arrives in fits and starts, and sometimes hits dead ends, more appealing. Our first chapter's inciting incident features a big fight, triggered by a tiny insult. Pat starts the journey from jail, perhaps with a mentor. We alter the immediate objectives, embedded in Pat's inner dialogue, prior to later scuffles. More fights happen, some for good reasons, some for bad. Each time we expand Pat's view. Thoughts of avoidance, then peaceful resolution, creep in. Sometimes, it doesn't work; a punch is thrown. One time a push replaces a jab and so forth. Pat changes, step by step, via these goal directed choices. A new Pat emerges by the story's end. That's an arc.

Learning About Others

Scientific research concerning how humans learn about others helps you implement arcs. We've covered how humans relate to fictional characters as real people. This research reveals how we know others through mental models. It led to an equation for constructing, as well as a plan to introduce, your creation. Now, we turn to how models grow and change, which is synonymous with how your character's identity shifts. This process drives familiarity as well as an arc's trajectory. The following two findings, one on how simulacra update and the other on how humans assign responsibility provide the last chunk of relevant person perception research. Together, they show how reading filters through the brain into reader models.

Updating Simulacra

The low level mental processes supporting learning about people serve humans' quest for meaning. This sentence exaggerates but only a bit. Keep the big picture — reader coming to know and empathize with your creation — in mind as we drill down into the supporting brain functions. The human mind continues to amaze, holding the hundreds or thousands of simulacrum which allow us to navigate social situations. On the other hand, we have difficulty paying attention. Your mind, like anyone's, thinks about one thing at a time. This may not seem true given all the buzzing in your head. However, that ability accrues from rapid switching not parallel processing. Lengthy monographs have been written on this topic. They, without going into a bottomless rabbit hole, boil down to one applicable finding: as soon as you pay attention to something else, what had your attention fades back into memory. Besides hammering on avoiding confusion and boredom, this limitation informs an appreciation of reader learning.

There are two terms to learn about learning: online processing and updating. Online processing borrows a concept from computers: our brains load what we're paying attention to from memory into mind. Put another way, we activate a memory, in this case a simulacrum, to think about it. (We saw stereotypes do this in Chapter Four.) The activation may be very brief, microseconds, before the brain moves on. Further, what goes back into memory may not be the same. Incoming information can update, possibly improving or expanding the character model. We could recast the whole Golden Chain in these terms. Focus on the update that follows witnessing an incorrect prediction. Let's look back at Pat's sample arc. The simulacrum activates before every potential fight. Then, it updates every time a predicted fight fails to occur. This update includes any conclusions drawn from the situation, such as Pat is starting to think

about consequences or is getting soft. The update can also summarize reflections on Pat's history and links to other memories which online processing, i.e. active thought, produced.

The updates ensure the reader's model captures Pat's changing identity at each point. Readers know your character from these snapshots. They're a new being, to some degree, after each update. Orchestration demands controlling these changes and directing them toward the final identity. The updating process also reminds us that the words we write affect the reader's model indirectly. Recall impression formation creates the first version of the corresponding simulacrum. From this instant, the character grows or changes with every choice, but only if readers learn from that action. And, you must tread carefully; missteps can trigger the pernicious error avalanche. Poor construction forces the reader to patch together ill-fitting information. It's a recipe for failure. Effective orchestration demands continuity, where each tiny change ties to the next. It also demands the successive recharacterizations lead to a transformed (yet still integrated) being by your novel's end. In short, the auteur in you designs the character's trajectory as your craft transmits each step in words. The big picture change, from the being upon intro to your creation's final form, is the arc.

When creating an arc, keep in mind you seek empathy not knowledge. What readers pick up can be viewed as a byproduct of empathy enhancing choice. Overlap should increase with each sequential identity as your being and reader come together. Knowledge accretion, plus confidence from correct predictions, builds empathy. In addition, the steps taken along their trajectory regularly provide their own pay offs. These bonuses arrive outside of the golden chain. For example, the first time Pat

avoids bashing someone's head may produce an extra thrill from growth. It's hard to say exactly when they will happen; nevertheless, you should encourage them. The biggest bonus comes near the novel's end when the reader reflects on your being's progress. This change must extend your theme, but that topic lies outside our scope. Besides everything else it offers, the close of your story lets readers empathize with the final version. This space must prompt active thought. Induce, not heavy-handedly, the reader to see and appreciate how far they and the character have come on their journey.

Villains (and Heroes)

Related to arcs and stereotypes are the labels protagonist and antagonist. You also know them as heroes and villains. You may have noted a studious avoidance of these terms. We've concentrated on main characters, ones the story awards attention to, versus minors, who should remain one-dimensional and limited. Villainy doesn't fit neatly into this scheme. Creating successful characters, with our equation or otherwise, depends on their resemblance to real people, the authenticity a growing simulacrum signals. Traces of a good and bad permeate your multifaceted being. Then, the reader is left to judge their morality within the context you construct. In short, apply the "every villain is a hero in his own mind" adage and give your main character bad guy a well-developed arc, as well.

Take Advantage of Attribution Bias

Researchers have uncovered another useful quirk in how humans learn about others. Oddly, we are predisposed to making mistakes. This tendency toward error has negative consensus in real life; authors can take advantage of this pattern, called fundamental attribution error (FAE), to jumpstart learning. Let's explore. Remember we observe and build simulations to understand others and promote social success. In observing observation, scientists have found that humans regularly point to traits, such as personality, as opposed to contextual factors to explain behaviors. In other words, they overinterpret what they see to draw conclusions about identity as opposed to correctly analyzing what in the situation actually caused the behavior.

Turning to our crash test dummy, say a potential fight confronts Pat. A decision, to punch or not to punch, stems from a mix of internal and external factors. In running away, observers — including readers — are much more likely to attribute that choice to internal goals. Pat's a coward, feels guilty over past altercations and so on. These are traits, enduring patterns of identity. While busy overanalyzing Pat's psyche, the same observers tend to ignore external forces. Facts like Pat is tired or there are police watching have less weight in our calculations. There is one caveat. In understanding themselves the opposite bias appears. We nearly always use circumstances to explain our own behavior. Keep this in mind when setting up the courtroom trials taking place in readers' heads.

Our, possibly delusional, belief in agency supports attribution errors. Blaming the person, not the situation enhances our sense of control. In other words, "it's their own fault" readily displaces "they had no choice" when we make judgments. The lesson is human psychology predisposes readers toward drawing inferences about identity from choices. Conversely, if you don't want readers to update your character's identity, you have to overemphasize the circumstantial reason for their actions. For example, if Pat fails to rush into a burning building, FAE will increase the level of cowardice unless you go overboard and stress there was no possible way to go into that building. Even then, it will be hard for readers to not see this move as cowardly. As ever, test to see what a volunteer takes away from decisions when needed.

Plot Nurtures Your Character

Our spotlight on identity and choice in creating and developing *publishable* characters mandates creating a context conducive to those two, critical factors. You could say context is everything. Perhaps not, but it's vital. The same behavior against a different background will produce wildly different attributions. A sprinting Pat, for instance, could be headed toward a brewing fight or away. Circumstances affect interpretations and, hence, updates. Further, actions can't occur in a void. Either you provide the context required for actions to make sense and lead readers to desired conclusions, or the reader will create their own context to an unknown end. In short, stories require contextualized situations to progress. Context is vital from another angle, as well. The requirement for consistency, i.e. gradual change, means identity is less malleable than context. Put another way, your being brings a relatively fixed identity — rooted in past action — to a scenario. In contrast, you can engineer story elements to make that scenario's circumstances any genre-respecting thing you can dream up.

Contextualizing a situation comes more or less naturally; nevertheless proceed gingerly. You must convey everything your reader needs to understand what's going on. Recall how the investment retelling test enshrines this standard. The Golden Chain, then, lists the boxes to check to ensure sufficient info. In lieu of lengthy repetition, include the following list. First, explain what brought the character to this crossroads. Note that this part doesn't call for rehearsing backstory, only the immediate cause. Next, synchronize the character's identity. You and the reader must be on the same page as to who they are. In other words, the reader's fully-updated simulacrum must match yours. Finally, the moment of decision has to offer clear options and associated outcomes — also known as stakes.

This package fosters an identity-based decision from your being. Moreover, this set up leads to organic selection; your reader sees a consistent behavior, one driven by who they are. This approach avoids bad outcomes. Actions seen as originating in anything other than a being's illusory autonomy risk losing empathy. After the decision, the chain ends when your words spell out the immediate consequences. The aftermath should include an emotional response as well as any other effects that occur in the timeframe. As you'd expect, consider testing a chapter's pivotal decision to assess the reader's empathy as well as how their character model was updated. Please perform this test at least once in your authorial career. The results will surprise you. The volunteer's retelling of a decision is guaranteed to be eye-opening if not shocking. Even experienced authors miss details — the items on the GC checklist, which are essential to maximize empathy. These misses usually come from underestimating your audience's laziness and distraction. Keep in mind you read and revise with a much higher level of care than anyone else. Meanwhile, your customers read for pleasure. On top of this, empathy compounds. Repeatedly missing the mark postpones a deep connection. In contrast, squeezing the most out of every situation quickens full on grokking and winning your reader's love.

Context is Plot; Plot is Context

If contextualization comes naturally, stringing together situations into an arc provides the challenge. Concentrate, first, on making sure succeeding events are sensibly linked. This doesn't have to be unassailable cause and effect, i.e. event one inevitably leads directly to event two, but fallback on that if nothing more artful can be found. Sense, here, refers to the reader; they have to be able to follow your tale's progress. Put puckishly, continuity encourages them to continue while discontinuity is problematic (review Chapter Four). Recall, as well, being sensible assists readers' model building. After tying one event to the next, the next important step is to design and transmit your being's change. Setting up this identity evolution involves your story's beginning, middle and end. In more technical terms, an arc parallels the story, from an inciting incident, rising action, peak, falling action to resolution. Of course, you're familiar with this version of Freytag's Pyramid, a five-part story structure which, for good reason, is thought of as plot.

Plot, formally, sits outside of this guide's scope; nevertheless, its intimacy with character growth and change forces its consideration in this last section. To preview, the events that make up an arc's situations must align with its encompassing story. Permissible gaps only appear when you build multiple trajectories, which we will discuss later. In other words, arc and plot sync up for one character novels while those with larger casts take more care to integrate characters' trajectories into events. Unsurprisingly, plotting a one being story entails setting up sequential situations, each with appropriate contextualization, and then lining them up to support both knowledge accretion as well as a progression. The linear increase in knowledge is straightforward. You know your creature, have ranked their details' importance (Chapter Seven), and incorporate them into your writing. You can also track the development of readers' simulacra through testing anytime you want. Arcs, like plots, take more effort to structure because they need to accommodate the reader's emotions. In fact, curating the reader's experience is Freytag's pyramid's primary lesson.

Your audience embarks on an emotional journey, starting with the inciting incident. To digress, an inciting incident is a novel's first pivotal choice. So, it demands all the empathy inducing features that the Golden Chain lists. It also offers an additional dose of context to introduce the main character and world. Finally, it sets up the next major event, presumably in your second chapter. Stepping back, the relationship between your first two situations forms a vector, a directed line or arrow. Thus, the link between your inciting incident and the next event guides the rest of the story. The word launch fits because this arrow points the story to a particular trajectory. Conventional story structure, which you should respect (to avoid painful DNF), has energy increasing early in the trajectory. Hence, the rising action terminology. Of course, the story peaks or climaxes, after which energy slacks, the reader relaxes in the falling action and they get the resolution's closure.

Providing a satisfying experience calls for managing your audience's emotions throughout the journey. Again, you do this with words. For example, you set the story's tone, the speed with which it progresses and the cadence of events. Manipulating these and similar factors alongside your character's arc supports your overall goal: deep empathy. Success sees character and reader merging as they jointly act their way through an engaging ride. Of course, it's all fake. (Did you think it was real?) You constructed the experiences, above all the creature who supposedly made the choices. This truth doesn't take anything away from a great story's impact. Why? Because the reader actually goes on the journey in their imagination. In the same way we relate to fictional characters as real people, your audience takes an actual trip. Insert your favorite LSD joke here. That said, don't let the idea of management overwhelm you. Setting up and sequencing situations properly means the interaction between your character and their circumstances will generate the appropriate emotions.

In creating situations, the best advice repeats the overall lesson: make sure readers can and do relate to your beings as real people. Your scenarios' sole job is to provoke the behavior you want. You could object and see this as putting the cart before the horse, so let's trace this logic. FAE acknowledges every behavior is determined by internal and circumstantial factors. The internal is your creature's psychology, the aspect of their identity which drives choice, which you know. You also should know what you want them to do, the option that they'll select. (Recall it follows from your planned arc.) Thus, you need to pin down or build the circumstantial factors to foster an "organic" choice. Within this fill in the blank approach, consider yourself an auteur as you are with everything else.

Let's pause to talk about planning and its supposed opposite, known as pantsing (or gardening). The pantsing idea advocates having characters and worlds interact to produce a story. Then, the author "gardens" by cutting back or encouraging threads. In words attributed to a school icon, "I don't do outlines. I don't know what's gonna happen, I figure it out as I go." As you'd suspect, we unequivocally reject this view. Coherence, to support this point, requires careful orchestration. There's only two routes to a coherent story for loyal pantsers. First, they can retroactively enforce coherence after finishing a draft. This process works though it's a lot of work. Alternatively, they can know the story in advance, well enough to write it coherently the first time. Stephen King, not to disparage an all time great, appears to follow this pattern. To venture a hypothesis, his unrivaled skill includes the ability to work out intricate plots in his head. Most authors don't function at this level, and they don't have to. You can substitute planning for revision or having an inhumanly capable imagination. Another reason to plan, to have a clear story in mind (MCS, Chapter 5), is to exercise power responsibly — not for your character's sake but for your readers. For example, you control story time, compressing or expanding it as necessary. A life can be expressed in a sentence or a novel can tell the story of one lunch. Auteurs make these choices to please readers, being kind implies conscientiousness, i.e. having a plan.

Storytelling (and Genre) Conventions Govern Your Plot

In plotting your story, remember proper orchestration respects a type of inevitability in every character's trajectory. Think about throwing a rock; once you let go, you can be pretty certain about where it will land. Our concept of a story "template" grants the same kind of predestination to your being. Specifically, once you set an identity in motion with the inciting incident, the rest of their arc follows. Their arc climbs to the peak your launch prefigures and continues to the likely end. Put another way, a fully realized incident stamps what follows into a fairly rigid trajectory. Most importantly, the arc has to follow that particular path to achieve coherence. If the incident doesn't lead to the arc, then one of the two has to change. Let's entertain three first choices to illustrate. Recognize how each realizes its genre, then concentrate on how the first choice propels the story toward a pre-determined peak and conclusion.

All three illustrations start with Pat arriving home after a shift. The reaction to what greets them establishes the story. First, they may walk in on a spouse having an affair. Perhaps they storm out, setting up a divorce story, which peaks when the couple gets either back together or moves on. Alternatively, they could start crying (or murder), setting the stage for a personal growth arc which ends in a "better" (or dead) being. Second, they may storm in (or crawl) loudly complaining about their job. Anything from an argument to consolation arises, leading to a plan. Sticking to the genre gives us a range of possibilities from abandoning the middle class, where the character embarks on a new lifestyle, through knuckling under, where they may continue to work and complain, to a get rich quick scheme. The last has the star attempt to alleviate their problems by winning the lottery, for instance. Then, the formula has each option lead to a peak that will either affirm their decision or push them back to the old life, presumably wiser. Third, they may see an alien munching on the family pet. Whether comedy or horror, you can probably guess the peak and resolution. These simple sketches show how a first choice's unfolding consequences lead to a suitable plot.

Let's take this idea another step. Because every story element has to work together, a given character, world, conflict and theme almost dictate the plot. Of course, the same applies to any of four elements: committing to them severely constrains the fifth. Putting character first means their arc points the story in a general direction, and the incident pushes the plot down a unique path. Yes, there can be twists and turns but nothing twisty or turny enough to violate your genre or confuse your reader. Your job, from this perspective, is to engineer and execute this big picture through the MCS as you write. Then, revise to ensure that it's perfectly coherent before it reaches the reader.

Turning Situations into Plot

Plotting involves crafting situations and linking one to the next. Metaphorically, then, you're stringing pearls into a beautiful necklace. For a single character story, connecting these dots also executes an arc. Some semantics will help align this character-first approach to plotting terms you may know. First a caveat: these concepts seem to have wound their way into discussions on noveling from screenwriting, so they can lead you astray. For example, take the classic three-act structure. This template works great for stage plays and movie scripts but less well for novel-length fiction. Should you doubt this, try to find a great novel that peaks at the two-thirds mark. Our target is roughly 90 thousand words in 30 chapters, and the plot should peak around number 26 (85%). Keeping this warning in mind, here are some common terms and their application to what we've called situations.

First, events, which are units of plot. Thus, a novel's plot is its event sequence. We use events and situations synonymously, preferring the word situation due to the way it primes choice. Second, scenes; usually defined as units of plot action, again for our purpose, scene is synonymous with situation. Third, plot points, which are story events that substantially shove the narrative forward or change its course. Notice this definition turns on the magnitude of the change an event causes, so it's matter of degree not kind; specifically, a big change turns any event into a plot point. The emphasis this guide puts on incremental, cumulative change makes the idea of a plot point less useful for novel writers. Fourth, beats. Screenwriters generally take beats to be components of scenes. A beat is an individual act, such as a statement or an emotional shift, which shapes an unfolding situation. A beat, for example, could be a loud sigh, which conveys a creature's exasperation. Adopting a naturalistic writing style should make any situation's beats flow organically, so we won't worry about them.

Chapters, however, are vital; in our definition, they're an around three thousand word unit of reading. Great chapters do more than divide a novel into chunks; they regulate the story's transmission as it passes from your brain to the reader's. They also have a special function to fulfill, actually two functions. Each has to be satisfying. In other words, a chapter succeeds when its reading induces a smile, burp or more as if your reader has finished a good meal. Then, in tension with the first objective, a great one leaves the reader wanting more, specifically your story's next step. Seeing each chapter as a mini-story, meaning it delivers a singular emotional peak embedded within a choice situation, helps fulfill these two aims. It also helps to see them as short morality plays. As your reader experiences a chapter, the Golden Chain delivers vicariousness, consequences and eventual judgements. Then, these experiences coalesce into your novel, a story in which your character's arc as well as its emergent theme cause grokking.

Fun Is Other People

A final thought on context and plotting brings in a wonderful aspect to complete this guide. It may blow your mind. We've focused on constructing, transmitting and nurturing one main character. Now, let's use this knowledge to create more. Why? Other beings are a crucial part of your creature's context. Novels reflect human lives and, as we've seen, depend on brains equipped to navigate social life. Welcoming other main characters into your story rests on this core. It also opens countless doors. We're drawn to making sense of human interactions. Most writers find endless joy in making up stories about strangers they see. New cast members offer a neverending source of drama, i.e. conflict, which you can tap to construct situations. A simple logic holds that one character talks to themselves. The castaway or trapped astronaut, for instance, muses about their surroundings while slowly going crazy. Two characters more than double the avenues to explore; they interact with the world and each other. Three characters explode the possibilities (as you'll soon see). In fact, social dynamics produce the majority of situations in novels because they're easy to write and readers devour them.

Unsurprisingly, the treasure a larger cast yields comes with caveats. The central issue continues Chapter Four's separation of major from minor characters. Recall, major characters require focus and brain space to gain empathy. Minors, in contrast, serve as foils; they get cursory attention and scant empathy. This distinction saves you and the reader from spreading energy, including the capacity for grokking, too thin. Let's apply this point to your cast. First, you can add all the minors you want so long as they remain one-dimensional. (Crush any would be climbers.) Tread carefully with major characters, those whose addition reshapes the story. Every time you add another main you're slicing up the reader's mind pie, which risks each having too small a piece to achieve deep empathy. In a dual POV novel, for example, each star gets roughly half the attention and thought. Still, many great novels have two main characters; that said, some of their success comes from balancing their cast's treatment. The shares don't have to be half and half; instead, they must be proportional to the story while devoting enough words to each. Thus, second, spend time planning and judging before you add another being to your novel. Resist temptation until you succumb. Remember, every main character has to be central to the story, including everything we've covered: an intro identity, steady accretion and a full arc. And, they absolutely must induce grokking.

Drama Triangles

You may want firmer guidance as to how many characters to create. Here it is: three. Again, one character novels tend to bump along a linear adventure; as stated, arc and plot match. A one person show walks the line between intimacy, which can be very rewarding, and claustrophobia. Ben Franklin said "three can keep a secret, if two of them are dead." In other words, one being walks a lonely path, their secrets safe with the reader. Having two leads also has pros and cons. Imagine an obsessive couple alternately loving and fighting their way through the story in each other's arms. Relative to one being, interpersonal drama flies off the page. Many wonderful stories grow from this foundation; Batman and Robin and Romeo and Juliet (there's a title) to name two. Yet, there's a yet: duos also trundle along a relatively set path. To illustrate, stories start with them together or apart. If apart, a dual POV for example, the reader knows they will meet and devotes mindspace to anticipating that moment's hows and whys. After they meet, the story continues as if they were joined at the hip because their relationship dominates the story. Whether committed allies or suspicious frenemies, their attitudes and behaviors toward each other pervade every context. Put simply, partnerships are less complicated than other social structures, they tend to be a hundred percent or gone. Compelling partner stories, such as buddies, lovers and parent / child, abound, but taking this route compels you to respect the duo dynamic.

If two is too little and we don't want too much, the right answer is three. Having this many main characters creates a drama triangle. So much recommends this configuration that it has always been a narrative staple. Compared to one or two actors, the interactions between any triad is highly unstable and, thus, offer a wealth of possibilities. Recall it takes three to gossip. Political science devotees will know three players can never form a stable alliance system because the outsider will continually

try to break up any couple. (You can look to World War Two for an example.) This formula is guaranteed to ease writing and increase satisfaction. Let's go through a specific triangle to sketch the options.

Speaking of coupling, the widely used love triangle is the most accessible. These stories revolve around three beings whose individual quests for romance become entangled and a source of conflict. Step back to notice desire stems from their identities, which require the discussed construction for the story to succeed. At another level, notice anything can substitute for romance as the motivation, such as money or fame. A typical narrative has one being choosing between two others or, equivalently, two competing for the third. Because nobody can make a quick, calm choice (and stick to it), this structure presents a massive tree, full of potential storyline branches. Notable examples include *The Hunger Games* and the all time great, *Casablanca.*

A variation introduces a moral element to the triangle. A tighter focus on one character generally accompanies this shift. Respecting our previous thoughts about villains, the leading character has to choose between two sides, sometimes labeled good and evil. Hamlet has the titular character vacillating between Claudius and his father's ghost, for instance. Classic Star Wars has Luke trusting Obi-Wan and then Yoda while tempted by Vader and the Emperor. The thematic choice shows up in the triangle's personas. Personification lets action and dialogue take the place of exposition. Overall, having three characters dramatically increases your options for identities and contexts relative to two or one. We'll leave the issues caused by having four, let alone more, main characters for you to think about.

Multiple Main Characters Contexts

Recall every main character requires an identity (perhaps from the Character Equation), which provokes deep empathy in successful novels. Their identity functions through the goals it brings to choice situations and also serves as their arc's reference point. A situation with two main characters, thus, compels you to account for two goals and arcs. This abundance makes multi-main plots harder to construct even as they offer more investible dynamics. Let's view this task through the lens of building two, parallel, Golden Chains. We'll name the characters Pat and Sam for clarity.

First, choose which being is the vicarious experience partner. The options are to write from the POV of Pat, Sam, both or neither. Avoid neither; that's easy. Choosing both is intriguing though it involves more work to avoid confusion. Specifically, you think through the timeline (in addition to all else), and then write the scene in a way that maintains readers' orientation. Recall humans can switch mental tasks quickly, e.g. between their models of your characters. However, each switch runs the risk of disorientation, i.e. not being able to put themselves and the actors into context. Read your work aloud, at least, to test; if it's an important scene, consider using a retelling volunteer.

Selecting to write the scene from either Sam's or Pat's perspective presents the safest option. Still, you have to account for the other being's agency. One way, the most obsessive, to do this is to write the scenes twice from each being's frame of reference, going through the whole GC. (Of course, this also supports two character, overlapping POVs.) Then, you have the information needed to reflect the non-POV's behavior in the version that enters your novel. If you write Pat, for instance, the out character is Sam. It's too much to ask that you do this every time. Do it a few times to improve your craft. You also have to plan how the non-POV character will update when your audience reenters their mind. To illustrate, your reader is in Pat for the scene. Meanwhile, Sam can't be inert and so will make choices, including voicing opinions. When the reader rejoins Sam, whether in the same chapter or the next, an update occurs. Whatever happened will affect the Sam model.

Creating Main Character Dialogue

Your characters, as you're undoubtedly aware, interact mainly through dialogue. Our how to on authentic conversations appears here because it takes main characters to dialogue authentically. Shallowness marks your majors' interactions with minors; they are necessarily stilted, to say nothing of conversations between minors themselves. Recall that a lesser — literally — being's suppressed agency prevents them from contributing to the story on their own. Conversations with minor creatures should add to the reader's knowledge, by offering info on events, setting or circumstances, for instance. These occasions, however, largely exist to give your stars opportunities to act and to express themselves. Pat, for example, could punch a or walk away from a supporting player. (How did violence become the theme?). Main characters, on the other hand, have genuine interactions. Further, these authentic exchanges must progress the story. Repeat this: no wasted words.

We've gone over the realness of your beings, what it takes to make them authentic and inevitable, as well as agency. Extending these thoughts to dialogue, shows our usual two pillars in play: identity and context. Two talkers, thus, means two integrated, complicated models interacting within your constructed scenario. The primary objective is verisimilitude — a conversation that authentically reflects who they are in the instant. Put another way, what they say must emerge naturally from identity. Then, what some miss, the reactions to what's said must emerge in the same way. Recall, as well, readers empathize with one character at a time; this limits their appreciation of the "out" perspective. That said, readers will still measure what's said against the out character's identity.

How do you create this wonderfully appealing and easy-to-write dialogue? Past having the respective identities in mind, remember a clash of wants must take the wheel. Put simply, agreement is boring. Answering should we attack the castle with a resounding yes does not make good conversation. Start with the reason for the meeting, what brought the characters to the situation. They, for example, could bump into one another while shopping or be part of a formal corporate board meeting. This lead in, plus the circumstance info package described above, sets the stage for joint action. Then, pinpoint (and write down in larger block letters) their separate intentions — what does each character want? You may need to think extra hard to induce conflict. It's there; where two intelligent beings live, they can find something to argue about. So long as conflict follows from their respective identities, you're good to go.

Next, use this grounding to imagine the scene. What do your creations say first? The three main tactics in any social fight are bribery, force and persuasion. A would-be briber says I'll pay you to get what I want. They may offer a thousand dollars or a trade. You scratch my back, I'll scratch yours, for example. People naturally do things for rewards. More to the point, a deal may not be struck, and the pay off may not be made. You could, for instance, spend pages on bargaining. (Not too many) Force is similar. Do what I want, or I'll stab you. Or, they could threaten the family dog if they're truly evil. Persuasion is the toughest and yet the most interesting. You can apply the idea that all communication is persuasion. Trying to win someone over to your view is revealing, as well. This tactic lets you dig into the participants' motives — and emotions — as they hash things out. Of course, these three options contain innumerable variations. Most importantly, identity must govern the tactic you choose for them to employ. The angry version of Pat may be inclined to threaten, which shifts to bribery and persuasion as the story progresses. If you completed Chapter Six's identity work, an opening line should pop right out. If it doesn't, ask your puppet. If that doesn't work, time to go back and spend more time on development.

As important as opening lines are, what comes next really matters in terms of authenticity. As the saying goes, all acting is reacting; alternatively, everyone has a plan until they get punched in the face (courtesy of Mike Tyson). In short, you can't pre-plan dialogue and expect it to be organic; you should only plan the opening overture. A reaction comes next. In fact, a well-developed identity, properly contextualized, prompts an immediate, authentic response. Of course, said response may be a blank stare. Keep in mind readers will flag any identity inconsistencies. You can tell when dialogue works even as you know if it's off. Test to eliminate any doubts. Great dialogue leads to nodding and maybe a cheer. Squints or other puzzled looks are red flags. Worst-case, they turn and look at you because the words don't make sense. Subtlety works wonders. A flash of temper, for example, may be enough to convey Pat's reaction. Another being could crack a joke or cry. Finally, don't forget the stakes. Why does your character want what they want? Clear understanding, i.e. knowing your characters, empowers you to effectively convey their thoughts and feelings, so the reader will empathize. And, as you've learned, deep empathy wins love and enthusiastic fans.

Now, on to the Comprehensive Character Developer (last time: an interactive version is at https://bardsy.com/character)

Bardsy Comprehensive Character Developer

Chapter 09

Comprehensive Character Developer

an online, continually updated version of this developer is available at https://bardsy.com/character

Instructions

You want authentic, investable characters with whom readers deeply empathize. This developer embodies a proven approach to reaching this goal. It's mostly self-explanatory (though some parts may challenge received wisdom). We encourage you to try it out, knowing that you can revise your being at any time.

The guide explains how readers relate to fictional people as if they were real through mental models called simulacra. Thus, in using this developer you're working toward constructing a simulacrum of your character to keep in mind as you write. The immediate goal is to know them well enough for their thoughts and behaviors to emerge organically.

Remember, compelling novels generally have three main characters with fully realized identities, and you can use the developer for each. Minor beings can remain as sketches (i.e., no need to develop). Overall, you should optimize the information you present to make it easy for readers, which loosely translates to cutting out any detail that isn't relevant to the story.

We recommend following these three steps before or while you write:

1. Use the Character Equation to compose a foundation.

2. Add specific, story relevant details.

3. Print, then interact with them to blend their aspects into an integrated being.

Begin with the Character Equation. Read the explanations and think about the three ingredients: pieces of you (the author), cultural knowledge, like stereotypes, and aspects of people you know (referents). If necessary, practice finding ingredients by decomposing a character from your favorite author.

After adding your ingredients, work through the other tabs to add specific, relevant details. Of course, judging relevancy demands knowing your story. Try not to pick too many and whittle them down when you're done. You should see that readers can't be expected to remember everything, but they'll add story significant details to their model of your character when they're situationally important. The inspirations are just that, examples to get your juices flowing.

When you're done, integrate the aspects you've selected into a human-like model through interactions. For example, hand the sheet to a friend, and ask them to roleplay. To learn more about blending and testing, we encourage you to reread this guide or come to a Bardsy workshop.

Let us know how you did, or make suggestions, below! And keep writing!

Essentials:

- Character Name:

- Nicknames:

- Functional Description:
- Character Equation: Your Being's Core Components

Pieces of You (Author Contribution)

All auteurs leave traces of themselves. Bend to this necessity and consciously extract a few aspects of yourself. Transplant those slices of thoughts and behaviors, like a sense of humor or love of music, into your being. Be precise and set conscious boundaries on your transfers to avoid self-indulgence.

Cultural Universals(Stereotypes / Archetypes):

Plan for your readers' contributions, which largely come from stereotypes and archetypes. Yes, stereotyping is bad, but readers do it anyway. This cultural knowledge will wind its way into your characters, mainly through embellishments that extend the details you provide.

Your job is to manage their additions through awareness by listing the stereotypes and archetypes you want to trigger. Also, be sure to list all that apply, and check your work by observing how readers see your creations.

Referents (Distinctiveness Stolen From People You Know):

Establish meaningful uniqueness with "referents." These are people (perhaps fictional), who you know well and can steal aspects from (this may be macabre, but it's effective). Again, be precise. Trace how certain intriguing features permeate their thoughts and behavior; then, steal those by listing them here for your recipe.

Physicality *Their observable looks and movements*

Appearance *What you generally notice about them*

Age As it seems…

- Oldest Person Alive
- Middle-Aged
- Numeric Age
- Teenager
- Immortal
- Child
- Adult

Height As it seems…

Weight As it seems…

Body Type As it seems…

- Narrow-hipped
- Chunky
- Muscular
- Serpentine
- Pear-shaped
- Barrel-chested
- Petite
- Well-endowed
- Ethereal

Skin Tone / Condition As it seems ...

- Leathery
- Flawless
- Olive
- Blotchy
- Scaly
- Translucent
- Pale
- Scarred

Hair Color / Texture As it seems ...

- Color (Brown / Black / Blonde / Red)
- Spikes
- Frizzy
- Wig
- Voluminous
- Bald
- Dyed
- Medusa
- Feathers

Ethnicity / Species Pseudo-genetic precursors

- Celestial
- Vampire
- Black
- White
- Mutant
- Yordle
- Dragon
- Asian
- Mixed

Presenting Gender As it seems ...

- Female
- Indeterminate
- Nonbinary
- Male
- Transitioning
- Feminine Presenting
- Androgynous
- Masculine

Face Shape As it seems ...

- Masked
- Round
- Heart-Shaped
- Nonexistent
- Asymmetrical
- Square
- Babyish
- Diamond
- Oval

Facial Characteristics **As it seems ...**

- Forked Tongue
- Unibrow
- Thin Lipped
- Double Chin
- Freckles
- Hooked Nose
- Heterochromia
- Third Eye
- Almond Eyes
- Birthmarks

Modifications **More alterable aspects**

- Multiple Limbs
- Proper Deportment
- Goatee
- Tattoos
- Piercings
- Scoliosis
- Scars / Bruises
- Perfumed

Health **Observable condition**

- Molting
- Fit
- Obese
- Pregnant
- Prosthetics
- Radiant
- Mucus-laden
- Anorexic

Movement / Sound *Observable behaviors*

Speech / Accent **Formulation of words & sounds**

- Lisp
- Booming
- Monotone
- Southern Drawl
- French
- Duck Quack
- Machine Generated
- Sing-Song Voice
- Pretentious

Habits Regular behaviors

- Shapeshifting
- Limp
- Heavy Breathing
- Messy
- Fluid Ejecting
- Clicking
- Mirroring

Quirks Involuntary behavior patterns

- Addict
- Humming
- Lip Licking
- Nail Biting
- Hiding
- Squinting
- Hair Flipping

Gait How they get around

- Head-in-the-Clouds
- Creeping
- Quick
- Clumsy
- Noisy
- Teleportation
- Ambling
- Nimble
- Pacing

Psychology *How they think and feel*

Mental World *Standard paradigms, emotional responses & mentality*

Credo / Belief System Philosophy of life, morality & religion

- Seeks Justice
- Love Everything
- Anarchy
- Buddhist
- Cultist
- New Age Mysticism
- Catholic
- Pursuit of Knowledge
- Nihilism
- Atheist

Mission / Motivation Purpose for living & doing

- Legacy
- Change
- Prove Themselves
- Fit-in
- Creative Compulsion
- Safety
- Hedonism
- Insecurity

Love / Hate What they protect or eschew

- Freedom
- Weakness
- Money
- Specific Others
- Winning
- Dogma
- Race / Class
- Beauty

Obligations / Commitments Their loyalties

- School Spirit
- Duty to Serve
- Noncommittal
- Family First
- Divided
- Survival
- Opportunistic
- Secret
- Oath Bound
- Faithful Partner

Self-Perception Sense of self & capability

- Humble
- Over / Underachieving
- Patronizing
- Self-assured
- Martyr Syndrome
- Vain
- Doubting
- Megalomaniacal
- Self-denying
- Guilty

Self Other Relations Attitude toward themselves & others

- Trusting
- Blames Self
- Washes Hands
- Forgiving
- Regretful
- Disassociates
- Zen Acceptance
- Judgemental
- Cycle of Abuse

Emotional Control Patterns in self regulation

- Pathologically Confident
- Reactive
- Awkward
- Defensive
- Empathic
- Mimic
- Impulsive
- Stuck

Emotional Intelligence As it seems ...

- Projects
- Enlightened
- Growth Oriented
- Socially dept
- Sacrificing
- Peter Pan
- Feigns Helplessness
- Level-headed
- Immature

Mental Health Disorders or state of being

- Body Dysmorphia
- Anxious
- Transcendent Resilience
- Catatonia
- Stable
- Positive
- Depression
- Swings
- Narcissism
- Delusional

Phobias As it seems ...

- Truth
- Heights
- Destiny
- Intimacy
- Insects
- The Dark
- Divine Abandonment
- Failure
- Public Speaking

Coping Mechanisms Mental patterns / reflexes used to protect self

- Avoidance / Denial
- Exercise
- Lashing Out
- Binge-Eating
- Meditation
- Creativity
- Self-Harm
- Talking
- Substance Abuse

Tastes *Favorites things, likes & dislikes*

General Preferences A few of their favorite things

- Dreads Musical Theatre
- Adores Pantone 448 C
- Listens to Vinyl
- Hates Junk Food
- Warm Weather
- Only Eats What They Grow
- Obsessive Hockey Fan
- Wine Lover
- Cannibal

Other People Who they seek or avoid

- Champions Underdogs
- Trauma Bonds
- Respects Strength
- Avoids Eccentricity
- Prefers Kindness
- Likes Intelligence
- Gravitates Toward Mystery
- Disregards Class
- Trusts Aliens

Interests / Hobbies Doings aside from work

- Hunting
- Graffiti Art
- Blogging
- Judo
- Dancing
- Puzzles
- Storm Chasing
- Beast Taming
- Woodcarving
- Roleplaying
- Skydiving
- Magic / Alchemy

Prize Possessions Things especially valued

- Uncompleted Map
- A Weapon
- Personal Diary
- Family Heirlooms
- Rare Fine Art
- Childhood Doll
- Musical Instrument
- Sacred Object
- Their Wooden Leg
- House / Land

Desires *Conscious & unconscious wants + plans*

Hopes / Dreams As it seems ...

- Win a Prize
- Become Fit
- Finish School
- Find Treasure
- Bucket List
- Conquer
- Get Promoted
- Be First
- Write a Novel
- Move to Paris

Relationship Goals Find or avoid / intimate or platonic

- Polyamorous
- Other Species
- Soulmate
- Non-committal
- Romantic
- Dominant
- Self-clone
- Unrequited Obsession
- Brood
- Casual
- Companion

Secret Plan Hidden Agenda

- Take Over the World
- Settle a Debt
- Fit In
- Insane Popularity
- Revenge
- Archetypes Cultural
- Be Admired
- Win a Love
- Fairytale Ending
- Transform
- Overcome Anxiety

Archetypes Cultural personality package

- Rebel
- Mentor
- The Warrior
- Castaway
- Caregiver
- Tempter / Temptress
- Wildcard

Five-Factor Model *Scales for predicting choices*

Extroversion Orientation toward others

- Shy
- Reclusive
- Town Gossip
- Socializing Energizes
- Friendly
- Gregarious
- High Information Output
- Antsy in Solitude
- People-pleaser

Neuroticism Level of worry & sensitivity to stress

- Stoic
- Anxious
- Jealous
- Well-adjusted
- Cynical
- Distrusting
- Perseverates
- Avoidant

Openness to Experience Attitude toward novelty

- Has no routine
- Failure to Plan
- On the Spectrum
- Staid
- Rigid
- Adrenaline Junkie
- Flexible
- Daredevil
- Experience seeking
- Agoraphobic

Agreeableness As it seems ...

- Easy-going
- Confrontational
- Fun to be With
- Cooperative
- Charming
- Competitive
- Positive Outlook
- Disruptive

Conscientiousness As it seems ...

- Self-centered
- Mindful
- Pragmatic
- Irresponsible
- Meticulous
- Perfectionist
- Observant
- Gestalt Thinker
- Sloppy

Skills / Abilities *Genetic or acquired*

Brains General intelligence

- Critical Thinker
- Interpersonal
- Spatial
- Quick Witted
- Linguistic
- Musical
- Naturalistic
- Logical
- Kinesthetic
- Brainiac

Talents / Knowledge As it seems ...

- Gourmet
- Pilot
- Polylingual
- Animal Talker
- Hacker
- Musically Gifted
- Wizard
- Psychic
- Healer
- Unremarkable
- Inventor

Accomplishments Claims to fame or success

- Won a Prize
- Giant Slayer
- Victorious in Battle
- Virtuoso
- Survived an Ordeal
- Extensive Experience
- Fabulously Wealthy
- Certificate / Degree

Sociology *Their relationship to others & the world*

Family *As it seems ...*

Parents As it seems ...

- Estranged
- Abusive
- Surrogate
- Parents in Cryogenic Sleep
- Biological
- Absent
- Self-made
- Adoptive
- Helicopter
- Orphaned

Siblings As it seems ...

- Siamese Twins
- Multiple Siblings
- Found Blood
- Estranged
- Identical Twins
- Foster Siblings
- Birth Clade
- Missing
- Half Siblings

Spouse / Partner As it seems ...

- Evil Ex
- New
- Married for Reasons
- Widowed
- No Communication
- Arranged
- Lifelong Single
- Estranged
- Divorced
- Polygamist
- Other Species

Children As it seems ...

- Adopted
- Separated at Birth
- Biological
- Surrogate Birth
- Unexpected Pregnancy
- Spawned
- Inherited a Child
- Godchild
- Stepchildren

Extended Family Relevant relations outside of nuclear

- Kissing Cousins
- Siblings of Parents
- Cousins
- Local Deity
- Patron
- Tribe
- Children of Siblings
- Living Ancestors
- Grandparents
- Enmeshed Family
- Detached Family

Extended Family Relevant relations outside of nuclear

- Kissing Cousins
- Siblings of Parents
- Cousins
- Local Deity
- Patron
- Tribe
- Children of Siblings
- Living Ancestors
- Grandparents
- Enmeshed Family
- Detached Family

Other Relationships *Influential roles besides family*

Lovers / Partners Romantic / sexual relationships

- Age-gap
- Affair
- One Breadwinner
- Victim
- Friendzone
- Triangle
- Childhood Sweetheart
- Unresolved Ex
- Toxic
- Opposites

Friends / Enemies As it seems ...

- Uncomfortably Affectionate
- Listener
- Sorority Sister
- Instant Hatred
- BFF
- Ritualistic Rivalry
- Ringleader
- Transactional
- Bonded
- Lifelong
- Bulldozer
- Imaginary

Animals / Pets Different species companions

- Pet Eagle
- Animal Advocate
- Familiar
- Bird Watcher
- Support Animal
- Cattle Rancher
- Cat
- Pack Hunter
- Dog

Authority Figures Respected people and otherwise

- Headmaster
- CIA Operative
- Tutor
- Sheik
- Czar
- Police
- Sovereign Monarch
- Priest
- Parent / Elder
- Justice League

Associates Other, relevant minor characters

- Stunt-double
- Mutual Friends
- Mentor / Mentee
- Lady-in-waiting
- Acquaintance
- Antagonist
- Wingperson
- Brotherhood
- Neighbors / Roommates
- Secretary
- Teammates

Social Identity *Themself in relation to others*

Stereotypes Cultural group memberships

- Teacher's Pet
- Nosy Neighbor
- Workaholic Boss
- Brave Firefighter
- Introverted Gamer
- Sarcastic Teenager
- Chatty Hairdresser
- Naive Alien

Citizenship Relationship to birthplace or naturalization

- Opposes Borders
- No Status
- Traveler
- Immigrant
- Naturalized Citizen
- Xenophobic
- Dual Citizenship
- Galactic Citizen
- Foreign Citizen
- In Hiding
- Patriotic

Politics Party affiliation or other political beliefs

- Corrupted Official
- Liberal
- Conservative
- Politics Hater
- Unaligned Politically
- Community Organizer
- Candidate
- Independent
- Politically Active
- Ideological Member

Religious Affiliation Commitment to organized religion or belief system

- Loss of Faith
- Baptist
- Cult Member
- Religious Leader
- Mosque Member
- Militant Atheist
- Dark Worship
- Liberal Churchgoer
- Missionary
- God
- Witchcraft
- Pilgrimage

Other Groups Other memberships

- Secret Society
- Labor Union
- Scouts
- Fraternity
- Culture
- Rock Band
- Mensa
- Social Circle
- Navy
- Tight Friends

Social Standing *Themself relative to peers / community*

Class Status Perceived standing compared to peers

- Fake
- Good Marriage
- Poor
- Royalty
- Clergy
- Petty Noble
- Oppressed
- Old Money
- Lower Middle
- Slave

Public Reputation Individual respect from society

- Outsider
- First Among Equals
- Condescended
- Enigmatic
- Admired
- Disconnected
- Shunned
- Climber
- Hero
- Union Organizer

Finances As it seems ...

- Retired
- Destitute
- Living the Dream
- Nepo Baby
- Billionaire
- Bankrupt
- Day to Day
- On Welfare
- Thrifty
- Comfortable

Sexual Attractiveness Including Charisma

- Repulsive
- Plain
- Wow
- Seductive
- Geisha
- Stalked
- Universal Attractiveness
- OK for Some
- Disproportionate
- 40-Year-Old Virgin

Cultural Approach Involvement in collective pursuits

- Revivalist
- Tourist
- Movement Leader
- Assimilator
- Multicultural
- Progressive
- Born in the Time
- Appropriator
- Traditionalist
- Contrarian

History *Past relevant to their identity, especially choices*

Notable Events *Pivotal prior happenings*

Life Event Timing When they events occurred

- Education / Graduation
- DOB
- Marriage
- Death
- Childhood
- Launch
- Birthplace
- Parenthood
- Adulthood
- Teen Years

Geographic Origin Residences, travels and so on

- Underground
- Appalachian Trail
- Small Town
- Shelter
- The Void
- Ancestral Lands
- Moon
- Another Universe
- Pilgrimage
- Never Left
- Cruise Ship
- European Vineyard
- Classified

Past Affiliations Former Associations

- Fraternity
- Secret Society
- Culture
- Mensa
- Scouts
- Tight Friends
- Labor Union
- Rock Band
- Social Circle
- Navy

Illnesses / Accidents Past issues that influence present

- Brain Injury
- Time Travel
- Hit by Car
- Hemophilia
- Amputation
- Tongue Cut Out
- Otherworldly Disease
- Polio
- Prolonged Stasis
- Bad Back

Skeletons in the Closet Hidden potential shames

- Cheating
- Secret Affair
- Robbery
- Has Superpowers
- Shoplifting
- Hoarding
- Heir to a Throne
- Embezzling
- Serial Killer
- Human Trafficking
- Despised Group

Past Occupations Work done

- Farmer
- CEO
- Mercenary
- Soldier
- Priest
- Paladin
- Artist
- Government Worker
- Medicine
- Cyborg

Defining Moments *Incidents with lasting impact*

Best / Worst Thing Choice with moral / ethical impact

- Stood Idly
- Stole from Family
- Saved a Life
- Left a Comfort Zone
- Profound Revelation
- Overcame Disease
- Religious Epiphany
- Attempted Harm
- Betrayed a Friend
- Murdered

Trauma Experiences affecting stability & trajectory

- Imprisoned
- Abused
- Bullied
- Assaulted
- Enslaved
- Witnessed Horror
- Survived Disaster
- Persecuted
- Kidnapped
- Solitary Childhood

Peak Moments / Failures Signal achievements or opposite

- Lost Business
- Left at Altar
- Award Winner
- Elected
- Accidental Discovery
- Fired
- Gang Initiate
- World Dominance
- Branded
- First Graduate
- Received a Promotion

www.ingramcontent.com/pod-product-compliance
Lightning Source LLC
Chambersburg PA
CBHW010351150626
46554CB00015B/2527

* 9 7 9 8 9 9 3 3 9 8 7 0 9 *